CW00391682

THE ROYAL COURT THEATRE PRESENTS

One For Sorrow

by Cordelia Lynn

One For Sorrow was the 2017 Pinter Commission.

One For Sorrow was first performed at the Royal Court
Jerwood Theatre Upstairs, Sloane Square, on Wednesday 20
June 2018.

One For Sorrow
by Cordelia Lynn

CAST (in order of appearance)

Emma **Sarah Woodward**
Imogen **Pearl Chanda**
Bill **Neil Dudgeon**
Chloe **Kitty Archer**
John **Irfan Shamji**

Director **James Macdonald**
Designer **Laura Hopkins**
Lighting Designer **Guy Hoare**
Sound Designer **Max Pappenheim**
Costume Supervisor **Helen Johnson**
Assistant Director **Milli Bhatia**
Casting Director **Amy Ball**
Production Manager **Marius Rønning**
Stage Managers **Heather Cryan, Fran O'Donnell**
Scenic Artist **Morwenna Holttum**

One For Sorrow
by Cordelia Lynn

Cordelia Lynn (Writer)

For the Royal Court: **Lela & Co.**

Other theatre includes: **Best Served Cold (Vault Festival); Believers Anonymous (Rosemary Branch); After the War (UK & International tour).**

Opera includes: **Miranda (Opera Comique, Paris); The White Princess (Festival d'Aix-en-Provence, France); you'll drown, dear (Manifest, Centquatre, Paris).**

Cordelia was part of the Royal Court Young Writers' Programme in 2012 and was the recipient of the Harold Pinter Commission 2017.

Kitty Archer (Chloe)

One For Sorrow **is Kitty's professional stage debut.**

Awards include: **Sir John Gielgud Charitable Trust Award.**

Milli Bhatia (Assistant Director)

As assistant director, for the Royal Court: **Instructions for Correct Assembly, Girls & Boys.**

As director, other theatre includes: **The Hijabi Monologues, My White Best Friend/This Bitter Earth [part of Black Lives Black Words] (Bush); I Have AIDS [Jerwood Assistant Director Programme] (Young Vic); Rats (Duffield Studio, National); EmpowerHouse (Theatre Royal, Stratford East); No Cowboys Only Indians (Courtyard).**

As assistant director, other theatre includes: **Lions & Tigers (Sam Wanamaker Playhouse); Cell Mates, Filthy Business, Luna Gale (Hampstead); The Quiet House (& Park), The Government Inspector (& tour), What Shadows (Birmingham Rep).**

As associate director, other theatre includes: **What if Women Ruled the World? (Manchester International Festival).**

Milli is Trainee Director at the Royal Court. She is an Associate Artist at the Bush Theatre and a Creative Associate at the Gate Theatre.

Pearl Chanda (Imogen)

Theatre includes: **Ink (Almeida/West End); Julie (Northern Stage); The Glass Menagerie (Nuffield, Southampton); The Angry Brigade (Bush); Crave, 4.48 Psychosis (Crucible, Sheffield); Two Gentlemen of Verona (RSC); Godchild (Hampstead); The Seagull (Headlong).**

Television includes: **Motherland, Endeavour, Arthur & George, Holby City.**

Film includes: **The Final Haunting, Mr Turner.**

Neil Dudgeon (Bill)

For the Royal Court: **Bliss, Fewer Emergencies, Mountain Language/Ashes to Ashes, Blasted, Waiting Room Germany, Talking in Tongues, No One Sees the Video, Road, Shirley.**

Other theatre includes: **The Homecoming (Almeida); Closer, Yerma, School for Wives (National); The Importance of Being Earnest, Richard II (Royal Exchange, Manchester); Crackwalker (Gate); Miss Julie (Oldham Coliseum); The Next Best Thing (Nuffield, Southampton); The Daughter-in-Law (Bristol Old Vic); Colliers Friday Night (Greenwich); The Changeling (Cambridge Theatre Company/tour); School for Scandal (West End).**

Television includes: **United, Midsomer Murders, Nativity, Life of Riley, Kingdom, Survivors, Silent Witness, Coming Down the Mountain, Roman's Empire, Sorted, The Street, The Lavender List, The Return of Sherlock Holmes, The Plan Man, Murder in Mind, Dirty Tricks, Messiah, Mrs Bradley Mysteries, Four Fathers, Tom Jones, The Gift, Our Boy, Breakout, Out of the Blue, The All New Alexei Sayle Show, Common as Muck, Fatherland, A Touch of Frost, Sharpes Eagles, Nice Town, Between the Lines, Resnick.**

Film includes: **Son of Rambow, Bridget Jones: The Edge of Reason, Breathtaking, Crossing the Border, Revolver, Fools of Fortune, Red King White Knight, Prick up Your Ears.**

Awards include: **Monte Carlo Television Award for Best Actor for Single Film (The Gift).**

Guy Hoare (Lighting Designer)

For the Royal Court: **In Basildon, NSFW.**

Other theatre includes: **Julie, The Deep Blue Sea, Here We Go, Strange Interlude** (National); **Winter, Wings, A Doll's House** (& West End/ BAM, New York), **World Factory, Far Away** (Young Vic); **Clarence Darrow** (Old Vic); **Roots, Serenading Louie** (Donmar); **Little Revolution, A Delicate Balance, Waste** (Almeida); **The Father** (Theatre Royal, Bath/Tricycle/West End/UK tour); **Othello** (Northern Broadsides/West End); **Be Near Me** (National Theatre of Scotland/ Donmar/UK tour), **Peter Pan** (National Theatre of Scotland/Barbican/UK tour); **Sleeping Beauty** (Citizens, Glasgow); **Going Dark** (Sound & Fury/International tour).

Dance includes: **Macbeth, The Odyssey, Dracula** (Mark Bruce Company); **Arthur Pita's Metamorphosis** (ROH/Joyce, New York); **Havana Rakatan, Vamos Cuba** (Sadler's Wells/ International tour); **Mischief** (Theatre Rites/UK & International tour); **Spring, Sigma, Meta, 4x4** (Gandini Juggling).

Opera includes: **The Firework Maker's Daughter** (Opera North/The Opera Group/ROH/UK tour/ New Victory, New York); **Jakob Lenz** (ENO); **American Lulu** (Young Vic/Scottish Opera/The Opera Group/Bregenz Festival, Austria).

Guy's work in dance has been seen all over the world and includes works by Rafael Bonachela, Christopher Bruce, Theo Clinkard, Dan Daw, Laïla Diallo & Mélanie Demers, Robin Dingemans, Shobana Jeyasingh, Akram Khan, Henri Oguike, Alexander Whitley and Ben Wright. He has also designed lighting for over twenty works in numerous seasons for English Touring Opera.

Laura Hopkins (Designer)

For the Royal Court: **The Pass, Love & Information, Breath Boom, Ballegangaire.**

Other theatre includes: **Terminal 3, Act** (Print Room); **The Divide** (Old Vic); **Misalliance** (Orange Tree); **Opening Skinner's Box** (Improbable); **The Grapes of Wrath** (Nuffield, Southampton); **Annie Get Your Gun** (Crucible, Sheffield); **Tosca** (Teatro della Muse, Ancona); **Lanark** (Citizens/Edinburgh International Festival); **The Oresteia** (Home, Manchester); **The Seagull, Doctor Faustus** (Headlong); **Troilus & Cressida** (The Wooster Group/RSC); **A Delicate Balance** (Almeida); **Othello** (Frantic Assembly); **Black Watch** (National Theatre of Scotland).

Awards include: **Critics' Awards for Theatre in Scotland Award for Best Design** (Lanark); **TMA Award for Best Design** (Doctor Faustus).

Laura is Associate Designer with experimental theatre companies Imitating The Dog and Buckle, purveyors of progressive working class entertainment.

Helen Johnson
(Costume Supervisor)

Theatre includes: **The Inheritance** (Young Vic); **Follies, The Hard Problem, London Road** (National); **We Are Here** (Jeremy Deller/14–18 Now); **The Haunting of Hill House** (Everyman, Liverpool); **Sinatra** (West End); **The Same Deep Water as Me** (Donmar); **Written on Skin** (Festival D'Aix en Provence/ROH); **The Yellow Wallpaper** (Schaubuhne, Berlin); **Carmen** (Salzburg Opera Festival).

Dance includes: **Song of the Earth/La Sylphide, Giselle** (English National Ballet); **Chroma** (Danish Royal Ballet); **Infra** (Polish National Ballet); **The Steadfast Tin Soldier, The Nutcracker** (Tivoli Ballet, Copenhagen).

Opera includes: **Wozzeck** (Lyric Opera, Chicago); **Between Worlds** (ENO); **Cosi Fan Tutti, Onegin** (ENO/Metropolitan Opera); **Die Frau Ohne Schatten** (ROH).

James Macdonald (Director)

For the Royal Court: **The Children** (& MTC/ Broadway), **Escaped Alone** (& BAM, NYC), **The Wolf From the Door, Circle Mirror Transformation, Love & Information** (& NYTW), **Cock** (& Duke, NYC), **Drunk Enough to Say I Love You?** (& Public, NYC), **Dying City** (& Lincoln Center, NYC), **Fewer Emergencies, Lucky Dog, Blood, Blasted, 4.48 Psychosis** (& St Anne's Warehouse, NYC/US & European tours), **Hard Fruit, Real Classy Affair, Cleansed, Ballegangaire, Harry & Me, Simpatico, Peaches, Thyestes, Hammett's Apprentice, The Terrible Voice of Satan, Putting Two & Two Together.**

Other theatre includes: **John, Dido Queen of Carthage, The Hour We Knew Nothing of Each Other, Exiles** (National); **Who's Afraid of Virginia Woolf?, Glengarry Glen Ross, The Changing Room** (West End); **The Way of the World, Roots** (Donmar); **The Father** (Theatre Royal, Bath/ Tricycle/West End); **The Tempest, Roberto Zucco** (RSC); **Wild, And No More Shall We Part, #aiww – The Arrest of Ai Weiwei** (Hampstead); **Bakkhai, A Delicate Balance, Judgment Day, The Triumph of Love** (Almeida); **The Chinese Room** (Williamstown Festival); **Cloud Nine** (Atlantic, NYC); **A Number** (NYTW); **King Lear, The Book of Grace** (Public, NYC); **Top Girls** (MTC/ Broadway); **John Gabriel Borkman** (Abbey, Dublin/BAM, NYC); **Troilus und Cressida, Die Kopien** (Schaubuehne, Berlin); **4.48 Psychose** (Burgtheater, Vienna); **Love's Labour's Lost, Richard II** (Royal Exchange, Manchester); **The Rivals** (Nottingham Playhouse); **The Crackwalker** (Gate); **The Seagull** (Crucible, Sheffield); **Miss Julie** (Oldham Coliseum); **Juno & the Paycock, Ice Cream/Hot Fudge, Romeo & Juliet, Fool for Love, Savage/Love, Master Harold & the Boys** (Contact, Manchester); **Prem** (BAC/Soho Poly).

Opera includes: **A Ring A Lamp A Thing (Linbury); Eugene Onegin, Rigoletto (Welsh National Opera); Die Zauberflöte (Garsington); Wolf Club Village, Night Banquet (Almeida Opera); Oedipus Rex, Survivor from Warsaw (Royal Exchange, Manchester/Hallé); Lives of the Great Poisoners (Second Stride).**

Film includes: **A Number.**

James was an Associate and Deputy Director at the Royal Court for 14 years and was also a NESTA fellow from 2003 to 2006.

Max Pappenheim (Sound Designer)

For the Royal Court: **The Children (& MTC/ Broadway); Ophelias Zimmer (& Schaubühne, Berlin).**

Other theatre includes: **The Way of the World (Donmar); Humble Boy, The Lottery of Love, Sheppey, Blue/Heart, Little Light, The Distance (Orange Tree); Dry Powder, Sex with Strangers, Labyrinth (Hampstead); Miss Julie (Theatre by the Lake/Jermyn Street); The Gaul (Hull Truck); Cookies (West End); Teddy, Fabric, Invincible (national tour); Toast (Park/59E59, NYC); Jane Wenham (Out of Joint); Waiting for Godot (Crucible, Sheffield); Cargo (Arcola); Commonwealth (Almeida); Creve Coeur (Print Room); Wink (Theatre503); Spamalot, The Glass Menagerie (English Theatre, Frankfurt); The Cardinal, Kiki's Delivery Service, Fiji Land (Southwark); Mrs Lowry & Son (Trafalgar Studios); My Eyes Went Dark (& Traverse), Martine, Black Jesus, Somersaults (Finborough); The Hotel Plays (Langham Hotel).**

Opera includes: **Miranda (Opéra Comique, Paris); Vixen (Vaults/international tour); Carmen:Remastered (ROH/Barbican).**

Radio includes: **Home Front.**

Max is Associate Artist of The Faction and Silent Opera.

Irfan Shamji (John)

Theatre includes: **Mayfly (Orange Tree); Weathered (Southwark); Hamlet (Kenneth Branagh Theatre Company).**

Television includes: **It's Me Sugar, Informer.**

Film includes: **Red Joan, Murder on the Orient Express.**

Sarah Woodward (Emma)

For the Royal Court: **Love & Information, Jumpy, Presence, Built on Sand.**

Other theatre includes: **Quiz, London Assurance (Chichester Festival/West End); Nell Gwynn (& West End), The Merry Wives of Windsor (& US tour), Richard II, The Comedy of Errors, Much Ado About Nothing (Globe); This House, The Curious Incident of the Dog in the Night-Time, Tom & Clem, Les Liaisons Dangereuses (West End); The Real Thing (& West End/ Broadway), Habeus Corpus (Donmar); Bracken Moor (Tricycle); The Cherry Orchard, The Hour We Knew Nothing of Each Other, Present Laughter, Wild Oats, The Sea (National); Snake in the Grass (Print Room); Judgment Day, The Rape of Lucrece (Almeida); Rookery Nook (Menier Chocolate Factory); Macbeth, A Midsummer Night's Dream, Romeo & Juliet, Arms & the Man (Regent's Park Open Air); Woman in Mind (Salisbury Playhouse); The Tempest, Love Labour's Lost, The Venetian Twins, Murder in the Cathedral, Henry V, Camille, Hamlet, Richard III, Red Noses (RSC); Artist Descending a Staircase (King's Head/West End); Angleus, From Morning 'til Night (Soho Poly); Talk of the Devil (Bristol Old Vic); The Winter's Tale (Birmingham Rep).**

Television includes: **Endeavour, Outnumbered, The Prime Minister's Husband, Loving Miss Hatto, The Politician's Husband, DCI Banks: Aftermath, Law & Order, Kingdom, Hear the Silence, Final Demand, Doctors, The Bill, Casualty, Gems, Poirot, New Tricks.**

Film includes: **Bright Young Things, I Capture the Castle, Doctor Sleep, The House of Angelo.**

Awards include: **Olivier Award for Best Supporting Actress (Tom & Clem); Shakespeare's Globe Classic Award (The Tempest); Clarence Derwent Award (Artist Descending a Staircase).**

THE ROYAL COURT THEATRE

The Royal Court Theatre is the writers' theatre. It is a leading force in world theatre for energetically cultivating writers – undiscovered, emerging and established.

Through the writers, the Royal Court is at the forefront of creating restless, alert, provocative theatre about now. We open our doors to the unheard voices and free thinkers that, through their writing, change our way of seeing.

Over 120,000 people visit the Royal Court in Sloane Square, London, each year and many thousands more see our work elsewhere through transfers to the West End and New York, UK and international tours, digital platforms, our residencies across London, and our site-specific work. Through all our work we strive to inspire audiences and influence future writers with radical thinking and provocative discussion.

The Royal Court's extensive development activity encompasses a diverse range of writers and artists and includes an ongoing programme of writers' attachments, readings, workshops and playwriting groups. Twenty years of the International Department's pioneering work around the world means the Royal Court has relationships with writers on every continent.

Within the past sixty years, John Osborne, Samuel Beckett, Arnold Wesker, Ann Jellicoe, Howard Brenton and David Hare have started their careers at the Court. Many others including Caryl Churchill, Athol Fugard, Mark Ravenhill, Simon Stephens, debbie tucker green, Sarah Kane – and, more recently, Lucy Kirkwood, Nick Payne, Penelope Skinner and Alistair McDowall – have followed.

The Royal Court has produced many iconic plays from Laura Wade's **Posh** to Jez Butterworth's **Jerusalem** and Martin McDonagh's **Hangmen**.

Royal Court plays from every decade are now performed on stage and taught in classrooms and universities across the globe.

It is because of this commitment to the writer that we believe there is no more important theatre in the world than the Royal Court.

Supported using public funding by
**ARTS COUNCIL
ENGLAND**

ROYAL

COMING UP AT THE ROYAL COURT

12 Jul – 11 Aug
Pity
By Rory Mullarkey

5 Sep – 13 Oct
The Woods
By Robert Alan Evans

21 Sep – 6 Oct
Poet in da Corner
By Debris Stevenson

Part of Represent, a series of artworks inspired by
the Representation of the People Act 1918.

Co-commissioned by 14–18 NOW: WW1 Centenary Art
Commissions and the Royal Court Theatre, supported
by Jerwood Charitable Foundation, in association with
Nottingham Playhouse and Leicester Curve.

25 Oct – 24 Nov
ear for eye
By debbie tucker green

Produced in association with Barbara Broccoli.

28 Nov – 12 Jan
Hole
By Ellie Kendrick

Part of the Royal Court's Jerwood New Playwrights
programme, supported by Jerwood Charitable
Foundation.

6 Dec – 26 Jan
The Cane
By Mark Ravenhill

Tickets from £12
royalcourttheatre.com

Sloane Square London, SW1W 8AS ⊖ Sloane Square
⇒ Victoria Station 🐦 royalcourt 📘 royalcourttheatre

ARTS COUNCIL ENGLAND
Supported using public funding by

JERWOOD CHARITABLE FOUNDATION

COURT

ROYAL COURT SUPPORTERS

The Royal Court is a registered charity and not-for-profit company. We need to raise £1.5 million every year in addition to our core grant from the Arts Council and our ticket income to achieve what we do.

We have significant and longstanding relationships with many generous organisations and individuals who provide vital support. Royal Court supporters enable us to remain the writers' theatre, find stories from everywhere and create theatre for everyone.

We can't do it without you.

PUBLIC FUNDING

Arts Council England, London
British Council

TRUSTS & FOUNDATIONS

The Backstage Trust
The Bryan Adams Charitable Trust
The Austin & Hope Pilkington Trust
Martin Bowley Charitable Trust
Gerald Chapman Fund
CHK Charities
The City Bridge Trust
The Clifford Chance Foundation
Cockayne - Grants for the Arts
The Ernest Cook Trust
The Nöel Coward Foundation
Cowley Charitable Trust
The Eranda Rothschild Foundation
Lady Antonia Fraser for The Pinter Commission
Genesis Foundation
The Golden Bottle Trust
The Haberdashers' Company
The Paul Hamlyn Foundation
Roderick & Elizabeth Jack
Jerwood Charitable Foundation
The Mackintosh Foundation
The Andrew Lloyd Webber Foundation
The London Community Foundation

John Lyon's Charity
Clare McIntyre's Bursary
Old Possum's Practical Trust
The Andrew W. Mellon Foundation
The David & Elaine Potter Foundation
The Richard Radcliffe Charitable Trust
Rose Foundation
Royal Victoria Hall Foundation
The Sackler Trust
The Sobell Foundation
John Thaw Foundation
The Wellcome Trust
The Garfield Weston Foundation

CORPORATE SPONSORS

Aqua Financial Solutions Ltd
Cadogan Estates
Colbert
Edwardian Hotels, London
Fever-Tree
Gedye & Sons
Kirkland & Ellis International LLP
Kudos
MAC
Room One
Sister Pictures
Sky Drama

CORPORATE MEMBERS

Gold
Weil, Gotshal & Manges LLP

Silver
Auerbach & Steele Opticians
Bloomberg
CNC – Communications & Network Consulting
Cream
Left Bank Pictures
Rockspring Property Investment Managers
Tetragon Financial Group

For more information or to become a foundation or business supporter contact Camilla Start: camillastart@royalcourttheatre.com/020 7565 5064.

INDIVIDUAL SUPPORTERS

Artistic Director's Circle
Eric Abraham
Carolyn Bennett
Samantha & Richard
  Campbell-Breeden
Cas Donald
Jane Featherstone
Lydia & Manfred Gorvy
Jean & David Grier
Charles Holloway
Luke Johnson
Jack & Linda Keenan
Mandeep & Sarah Manku
Anatol Orient
NoraLee & Jon Sedmak
Deborah Shaw
  & Stephen Marquardt
Matthew & Sian Westerman
Mahdi Yahya

Writers' Circle
Chris & Alison Cabot
Jordan Cook & John Burbank
Scott M. Delman
Virginia Finegold
Michelle & Jan Hagemeier
Chris Hogbin
Mark Kelly & Margaret
  McDonald Kelly
Nicola Kerr
Emma O'Donoghue
Mr & Mrs Sandy Orr
Tracy Phillips
Suzanne Pirret
Theo & Barbara Priovolos
Sir Paul & Lady Ruddock
Carol Sellars
Maria Sukkar
Jan & Michael Topham
Maureen & Tony Wheeler
The Wilhelm Helmut Trust
Anonymous

Directors' Circle
Mrs Asli Arah
Dr Kate Best
Katie Bradford
Piers Butler
Sir Trevor & Lady Chinn
Emma & Phil Coffer
Joachim Fleury
Piers & Melanie Gibson
Louis Greig
David & Claudia Harding
Dr Timothy Hyde
Roderick & Elizabeth Jack
Mrs Joan Kingsley
Victoria Leggett
Emma Marsh
Rachel Mason

Andrew & Ariana Rodger
Simon Tuttle
Anonymous

Platinum Members
Simon A Aldridge
Moira Andreae
Nick Archdale
Elizabeth & Adam Bandeen
Clive & Helena Butler
Gavin & Lesley Casey
Sarah & Philippe Chappatte
Andrea & Anthony Coombs
Clyde Cooper
Mrs Lara Cross
T Cross
Andrew & Amanda Cryer
Shane & Catherine Cullinane
Matthew Dean
Sarah Denning
Cherry & Rob Dickins
Denise & Randolph Dumas
Robyn Durie
Mark & Sarah Evans
Sally & Giles Everist
Celeste Fenichel
Emily Fletcher
The Edwin Fox Foundation
Dominic & Claire Freemantle
Beverley Gee
Paul & Kay Goswell
Nick & Julie Gould
The Richard Grand Foundation
Jill Hackel & Andrzej Zarzycki
Carol Hall
Peter & Debbie Hargreaves
Sam & Caroline Haubold
Mr & Mrs Gordon Holmes
Damien Hyland
Amanda & Chris Jennings
Ralph Kanter
Jim & Wendy Karp
David P Kaskel
  & Christopher A Teano
Vincent & Amanda Keaveny
Peter & Maria Kellner
Mr & Mrs Pawel Kisielewski
Rosemary Leith
Mark & Sophie Lewisohn
Kathryn Ludlow
The Maplescombe Trust
Christopher Marek
  Rencki
Frederic Marguerre
Mrs Janet Martin
Andrew McIver
David & Elizabeth Miles
Jameson & Lauren Miller
David Mills
Barbara Minto
M.E. Murphy Altschuler
Siobhan Murphy
Peter & Maggie Murray-Smith

Sarah Muscat
Georgia Oetker
Crispin Osborne
Andrea & Hilary Ponti
Greg & Karen Reid
Nick & Annie Reid
Paul & Gill Robinson
Corinne Rooney
William & Hilary Russell
Sally & Anthony Salz
Anita Scott
Bhags Sharma
Dr. Wendy Sigle
Andy Simpkin
Paul & Rita Skinner
Brian Smith
John Soler & Meg Morrison
Kim Taylor-Smith
Mrs Caroline Thomas
Alex Timken
The Ulrich Family
Monica B Voldstad
Arrelle & François Von Hurter
Mr N C Wiggins
Anne-Marie Williams
Sir Robert & Lady Wilson
Anonymous

**With thanks to our
Friends, Silver and Gold
Members whose support
we greatly appreciate.**

DEVELOPMENT COUNCIL
Piers Butler
Chris Cabot
Cas Donald
Sally Everist
Celeste Fenichel
Tim Hincks
Emma Marsh
Anatol Orient
Andrew Rodger
Sian Westerman

Our Supporters contribute to
all aspects of the Royal Court's
work including: productions,
commissions, writers groups,
International, Young Court,
creative posts, the Trainee
scheme and access initiatives
as well as providing in-kind
support.

**For more information or
to become a Supporter
please contact Charlotte
Cole: charlottecole@
royalcourttheatre.
com/020 7565 5049.**

Supported using public funding by
**ARTS COUNCIL
ENGLAND**

Royal Court Theatre
Sloane Square,
London SW1W 8AS
Tel: 020 7565 5050
info@royalcourttheatre.com
www.royalcourttheatre.com

Artistic Director
Vicky Featherstone
Executive Producer
Lucy Davies

Associate Directors
**Lucy Morrison,
Hamish Pirie,
John Tiffany*,
Graham Whybrow***
Associate Designer
Chloe Lamford*
Associate Playwright
Simon Stephens*
Trainee Director
Milli Bhatia+

International Director
Elyse Dodgson
Associate Director
(International)
Sam Pritchard
International Administrator
Rachel Toogood*

General Manager
**Catherine
Thornborrow**
Producer (Maternity Leave)
Minna Sharpe
Producer (Maternity Cover)
Ros Terry
Producer
Chris James
Assistant to the Artistic
Director & Executive
Producer
Romina Leiva Ahearne
Administration & Producing
Assistant
**Geraldine Alleyne
Vaughan§**

Head of Participation
Vishni Velada-Billson
Young Court Manager
Romana Flello
Young Court Workshop
Leader
Ellie Fulcher
Young Court Administrator
Vicky Berry*
Young Court Assistant
Jasmyn Fisher-Ryner‡

Literary Manager
Chris Campbell
Deputy Literary Manager
Louise Stephens
Literary Assistant
Ellie Horne

Head of Casting
Amy Ball
Casting Co-ordinator
Arthur Carrington
Casting Assistant
Monica Siyanga§

Head of Production
Marius Rønning
Production Manager
Marty Moore
Company Manager
Joni Carter
Production Assistant
Alysha Laviniere§
Deputy Head of Lighting
Matthew Harding
Lighting Technicians
**Cat Roberts, Eimante
Rukaite**
Head of Stage
Courtland Evje
Deputy Head of Stage
TJ Chappell-Meade
Stage Show Technician
Ben Carmichael
Head of Sound
David McSeveney
Deputy Head of Sound
Emily Legg
Head of Costume
Lucy Walshaw
Wardrobe Manager
Gina Lee

Finance Director
Helen Perryer
Financial Controller
Edward Hales
Finance Officer
Lewis Kupperblatt
Accounts Assistant
Anais Pedron*
Finance & Administration
Assistant
Catherine Kirk

Head of Press & Publicity
Anoushka Warden
Press Assistant
Jonathan Oakman

Head of Marketing & Sales
Holly Conneely
Marketing Manager
Dion Wilson
Marketing Officer
Candace Chan
Marketing Assistant
Frankie Wakefield§

Sales & Ticketing Manager
Farrar Hornby
Deputy Sales Manager
Ava Eldred
Box Office Sales Assistants
**Samuel Bailey*,
Eleanor Crosswell*,
Caitlin McEwan,
Margaret Perry***

Development Director
Lucy Buxton
Head of Individual Giving
Charlotte Christesen
Head of Trusts
Bryony Mills
Corporate Development
Manager
Emma-Jane Ball
Development Officer
Camilla Start
Development Officer
Charlotte Cole
Development Assistant
Alejandro Librero§

Theatre Manager
Rachel Dudley
Front of House Manager
Adam Lawler
Duty House Managers
**Flo Bourne*,
Rhiannon Handy*,
Elinor Keber,
Tristan Rogers***,
Caretaker
Jimi Keyede*

Bar & Kitchen Manager
Robert Smael
Bar & Kitchen Supervisors
**Jemma Angell*,
Joel Ormsby***
Head Chef
David Adams
Sous Chef
Mateusz Trelewicz
Demi Chef de Partie
Nicusor Peretaneau

Stage Door/Reception
**Paul Lovegrove,
Dominika Mari*, Fiona
Sagar***

Manager of Samuel French
Bookshop at the Royal Court
Theatre
Simon Ellison
Bookshop Assistant
Terry McCormack*

Thanks to all of our Ushers
and Bar & Kitchen staff.

§ Posts supported by
The Sackler Trust
Trainee Scheme.

‡ The post of Young Court
Trainee is supported by the
Austin & Hope Pilkington
Trust.

+ The post of Trainee
Director is supported by
Cas Donald and Mandeep &
Sarah Manku.

* Part-time.

**ENGLISH STAGE
COMPANY**

President
**Dame Joan Plowright
CBE**

Honorary Council
**Sir Richard Eyre CBE
Alan Grieve CBE
Phyllida Lloyd CBE
Martin Paisner CBE**

Council Chairman
Anthony Burton CBE
Vice Chairman
Graham Devlin CBE
Members
**Jennette Arnold OBE
Judy Daish
Sir David Green KCMG
Noma Dumezweni
Joyce Hytner OBE
Stephen Jeffreys
Emma Marsh
Roger Michell
James Midgley
Anita Scott
Lord Stewart Wood
Mahdi Yahya**

"There are no spaces, no rooms in my opinion, with a greater legacy of fearlessness, truth and clarity than this space."

Simon Stephens, Associate Playwright

The Royal Court invests in the future of the theatre, offering writers the support, time and resources to find their voices and tell their stories, asking the big questions and responding to the issues of the moment.

As a registered charity, the Royal Court relies on the generous support of individuals to seek out, develop and nurture new voices. Please join us in Writing The Future by donating today.

You can donate online at royalcourttheatre.com/donate or via our donation box in the Bar & Kitchen.

We can't do it without you.

Writing the Future

To find out more about the different ways in which you can be involved please contact Charlotte Cole on 020 7565 5049 / charlottecole@royalcourttheatre.com

The English Stage Company at the Royal Court Theatre is a registered charity (No. 231242).

ONE FOR SORROW

Cordelia Lynn

One for sorrow
Two for mirth
Three for a funeral
Four for birth
Five for heaven
Six for hell
Seven for the devil,
His own self.

Characters

EMMA, *mid-fifties*
IMOGEN, *early twenties*
BILL, *early fifties*
CHLOE, *late teens*
JOHN, *mid-twenties*

Scene

A home.

Today, now.

Notes

/ Indicates an external interruption

– Indicates an internal interruption

… Indicates a tailing off

The television is as much a character as anyone else.

This text went to press before the end of rehearsals and so may differ slightly from the play as performed.

Prologue – In Darkness

An explosion

house lights out

screams confusion

shouting

gunfire

more screams running gunfire

a second explosion

screams

sirens

debris

JOHN'S VOICE I am outside.

> I am outside on the street and the air is hot with
> fear. The air is buzzing and hissing with fear and
> the fear is hot on my skin. The fear is desert hot
> and the fear is cooking my sweat.

> There is a lot of sweat.

> I am outside on the street and I am running. I am
> running outside on the street in the sand hot fear

and my backpack is heavy. My backpack is heavy and my backpack is weighing me down and pulling me back but I am strong and I am fast and I am running all the same.

Outside on the street. Tonight.

Now.

I am running outside on the street with my backpack and the fear in the air is cooking my sweat and I am running across this part of the city and I am running across the city to you.

Now.

Because you say, it is you that says, Come here.

Come here now. I will keep you safe.

Come right here now to us.

Tonight.

It is you that said it.

.

Didn't you?

I am walking in a residential area under the trees. The trees are lovely and cool and drink up the fear so the air is now lovely and cool. And my backpack is heavy and my heart is heavy and the air is cool but my heart is hot.

And I am outside on the street and I am walking to you. I am walking through this residential area and I am making my way to you. Now.

Because it was you that said, One day they will say that this was human nature.

Didn't you?

I am at your door now. I am at your door now
outside tonight on the street in this residential area.
I am knocking at your door. I am knocking at your
door and I say, Let me in Let me in Let me in.

I need more time.

Let me in.

I am coming across this city to you. I am coming.

I am at your door and your door is open.

Expect me.

ACT ONE

Scene One

Lights up.

A house. Comfortable, modern. Art. Books. That sort of thing.

A living/dining space. A dining table, an unfinished meal. Wine. Chairs pushed back.

Back, centre, a hallway to the front door. Off the hallway a bathroom, and a staircase to the upper floor.

Off the main room, a kitchen. Also off, a sitting room with a television. The television is on.

A white family.

EMMA, IMOGEN *and* BILL.

EMMA	Because you cannot just /
IMOGEN	Listen to me /
EMMA	You cannot just /
IMOGEN	Listen to me /
EMMA	No you listen to me! For once you listen to /
IMOGEN	But you're not hearing me /
BILL	Listen to your mother, Imogen.
EMMA	Oh shut up, Bill!
IMOGEN	You're not hearing me /
EMMA	I am hearing you. We are hearing you. I've heard you loud and clear and you're completely out of control /
IMOGEN	I am not out of /
EMMA	You're completely out of control. This is completely out of /

IMOGEN	It's not out of /
EMMA	You've taken it too far this time /
BILL	You have taken it too far.
EMMA	I am patient with you, I am patient with the things you believe, I believe
	I believe in the things you believe /
IMOGEN	No you don't you don't /
EMMA	I'm talking now.

EMMA I am patient with you. I'm encouraging of you. But this is too much. This is this is –

You've endangered us.

IMOGEN	I haven't endangered us /
EMMA	You've endangered your family /
IMOGEN	I haven't endangered our family /
EMMA	Your sister, your little sister /
IMOGEN	She wanted me to do it. She agrees with /
EMMA	Of course she does! She's a teenager. They're all mad. You have no understanding of /
IMOGEN	I don't claim to have any understanding of /
EMMA	No understanding of the dangers. At a time like this, to do such a thing at a time like a time like /
IMOGEN	The danger is in your head, you need to hear me, it's all in your head /
EMMA	It is not in my head! (*To* BILL.) Tell her it is not in my head.
BILL	You only had to ask us and then we could have discussed it / reasonably.
IMOGEN	Reasonably.

BILL   We have to discuss these things reasonably. Why didn't you just ask?

IMOGEN   Because you're afraid. You're afraid of everything. You're afraid.

EMMA   Well perhaps when you're my age you'll know there are some things in life worth being afraid of.

IMOGEN   No. Not like that. I'm not afraid of anything like that. Because fear is –

          Your fear, the fear you have is just an excuse to do terrible things, and to do nothing. Which is also a terrible thing.

          Pause.

EMMA   Right. I'm confiscating your phone /

IMOGEN   What?

EMMA   I'm confiscating your phone. I'm confiscating your laptop /

IMOGEN   You can't!

EMMA   Oh yes I can!

IMOGEN   It's a breach of my human rights /

EMMA   You want to talk to me about human rights? You want to talk to me about human rights?

IMOGEN   Not your kind of rights /

EMMA   Alright let's talk about human rights /

IMOGEN   Not your definition of /

EMMA   Let's talk about the Universal Declaration of Human Rights. Let's talk about the European Convention on Human Rights /

IMOGEN   Not those rights /

EMMA   Have you read the European Convention on Human Rights? Have you read the Universal Declaration of Human Rights?

IMOGEN   Not those /

EMMA   Well I have! And I interpret and advise on the European Convention on Human Rights every day, every day I /

IMOGEN   Western declarations on human rights are Neocolonial, Imperialist projects.

EMMA   I'm going to kill her. I'm going to kill my daughter. Bill, I'm going to have to kill our daughter /

BILL   Right. Well that's /

EMMA   A Neocolonial Project! A Neocolonial Project!

IMOGEN   You think you know everything. You think you understand everything. But you don't know anything. You're old, and you're afraid of everything.

It's not your fault. They made you afraid. You're not bigger than the culture you were born in to, and it made you afraid.

Pause.

EMMA   My life. My entire life, my legal career has been dedicated to –

I think I'm going to cry. I'm either going to cry or I'm going to murder our daughter.

BILL   Right. Well. Let's all just /

EMMA   What Bill? What should we all just?

Enter CHLOE, *from television room.*

CHLOE   45.

If you're interested.

I mean I'm just saying. I'm literally just keeping you guys updated with what's going on outside while you all just shout in here. That's just literally what I'm doing.

Because outside shit's really hit the fan and it's not
getting any better so I think you should just know
that it's

45. And counting.

Pause.

EMMA   Did you hear

have you heard from Elizabeth yet?

CHLOE   No.

EMMA   Right.

CHLOE   Her phone's off.

BILL   Perhaps she ran out of battery.

EMMA   That's right, perhaps she ran out of battery.

BILL   I'm sure she's fine. We'll hear soon that /

CHLOE   I just wanted you to know that it's 45 now.

And counting.

And I'm not mad just because I'm a teenager. And
actually calling people mad like that is ableist.

Exit CHLOE, *TV room.*

BILL   Right. So we're all just going to /

EMMA   Oh good, Bill is going to decide what we're all
just going to do /

BILL   I'm not going to /

EMMA   The man of the house is going to decide /

BILL   I'm not

that's not /

IMOGEN   She's right. You don't decide that.

BILL   Right. Okay.

IMOGEN   You don't get to decide that /

BILL   Right! I said right!

IMOGEN   Ever.

            BILL *knocks a chair over, backhand.*

            The women don't react.

            Pause.

BILL   Sorry.

            He picks up the chair.

            Sorry. I'm sorry. That was inexcusable.

            But you do gang up on me /

EMMA   Oh for god's /

BILL   You do. You shift allegiances /

IMOGEN   Allegiances? /

BILL   Just like that. And I'm trying to keep up and be
            fair but /

EMMA   You were going to tell us to calm down /

BILL   I was not going to /

EMMA   You were going to tell us to calm down and that
            is not /

BILL   I was not going to /

EMMA   You were going to /

BILL   Alright I was going to but not /

EMMA   So you see /

BILL   But not like that.

EMMA   Not like what?

BILL   I want us all to be calm. I want us all, myself
            included, to be calm so we can discuss this /

IMOGEN   Reasonably.

BILL   That is not a dirty word.

IMOGEN   It is.

BILL   It is not a /

IMOGEN   Yes it is a /

BILL   It is an important word. You cannot dispense with, it's the end of civilisation if you dispense with /

IMOGEN   In this context, you, us, and the weight of history, it is a dirty word. And you don't get to say that /

BILL   We've gone off-topic. As usual, we have gone off-topic /

IMOGEN   You don't get to say that either /

BILL   I'm being no-platformed. I'm evidently being no-platformed in my own house. Your generation is completely incapable /

IMOGEN   My generation!

BILL   You're completely incapable of having a /

IMOGEN   Reasonable discussion.

BILL   Well exactly!

IMOGEN   Okay.

BILL   We brought you up to be intelligent, to be able to have intelligent discussions, to

to think critically, objectively, to stand your ground /

IMOGEN   My ground? What ground?

BILL   And to know when you're wrong, and surrender your ground gracefully /

IMOGEN   I hate your language. I hate it. Like a conversation is an invasion, like we're at war.

BILL   Have you been watching the news? We are at war.

IMOGEN   That's hysterical. You're hysterical /

BILL   I am not hysterical /

IMOGEN   You are. You're hysterical.

BILL   There are bombs in the street tonight. There are dead people. There are men with guns. And you're telling me we're not at war?

IMOGEN   The war is in your head /

BILL   It is quite literally happening! Literally in the correct sense of the word, not in the sense that your lot throw it about the place like like

    fucking

    hundreds and thousands!

EMMA   What? (*Laughs*.)

BILL   Don't laugh at me! This is serious. It is literally happening outside and she's telling me, she's telling us, that it is not happening and it is in my head! (*To* IMOGEN.) Are you insane? (*To* EMMA.) She's insane.

    Enter CHLOE.

CHLOE   51.

    Just so you know. 51 now.

    And counting.

    And calling Immy insane like that is actually ableist.

    Exit CHLOE.

    Pause.

EMMA   Right. Right right right.

    51.

Right.

Pause.

Imogen. You are going to explain to me /

BILL   To us /

EMMA   To us. You are going to explain to us again, from the beginning /

BILL   Without jargon /

IMOGEN   It's not jargon! /

EMMA   You are going to explain to us both again, from the beginning, without jargon, exactly what it is you've done and why.

IMOGEN   I want to explain. I've been trying to explain.

EMMA   Good. That's good. Collect yourself. Think about it.

Take your time /

IMOGEN   It's just a hashtag.

It's just. A hashtag. It's just a hashtag that says Open Door. That's all it is. And that's all I've done. I've used that hashtag, I've shared that hashtag and –

That's it.

And all it means

all it means is that now, with everything that's going on now, outside

with everything that's happening out there tonight, that our door is open. All it means is that we understand that people are scared, that they might be trapped or hurt, that they might not be able to get home or –

And so we're saying to them, We are here. Come to our house. We'll look after you. You'll be safe. Our door is open.

> That's all it is.
>
> It's nothing to be afraid of.

EMMA   We're not afraid of the hashtag. It's not the hashtag
            we're afraid of. Or what the hashtag represents /

BILL   No, we're not afraid of what the hashtag
            represents.

EMMA   We are actually in favour of what the hashtag
            represents /

BILL   That's true, we are technically in favour of what
            the hashtag represents /

EMMA   And we are proud of you, we're proud of your –

BILL   We are proud of your humanity.

EMMA   We are. We are proud of your humanity. We
            brought you up to be humane /

BILL   Exactly.

EMMA   We're afraid of. What we are afraid of is what
            might happen if you share our address, on a night
            like this, during a terrorist attack, on social media.

IMOGEN   I have not 'shared our address on social media'.
            They have to contact me privately to get our
            address and I have not given anyone our address.

EMMA   Okay. That's good. That's very /

IMOGEN   And I don't think you should call it a terrorist
            attack.

EMMA   You what, Imogen?

IMOGEN   I don't think you should call it a terrorist attack.
            I don't think

            that you should.

EMMA   And why shouldn't we call it a terrorist attack?

IMOGEN   Because we don't know if it is yet and /

BILL   Are you telling me, are you telling me are you
            seriously trying to tell me that that

            bombs, explosions people dead on the on the people
            dead and dying on the street and guns and and

            and you're trying to tell me that it's not a terrorist
            attack!

IMOGEN   This is what I mean, this is exactly what I mean.
            Your language, your fear, your behaviour in the
            world, it's all connected. Because you jump to
            these conclusions, you do, you do all the time.
            Everyone, you, your generation, your media, your
            governments, you've created this world where
            everyone's so afraid, everyone's so afraid they
            can't even breathe any more because if you
            breathe it's toxic, it'll kill you, so you're all just
            walking around holding your breath waiting the
            whole time, just waiting for something to happen
            so you can start screaming and start killing
            because that's what you do it is

            what you do.

            Listen to me, it's what you do and it's what you've
            done.

            And I'm not saying it's not a terrorist attack, I'm
            not saying that at all, but I'm just not going to
            decide it is until it's confirmed because I'm not
            going to use that language and I'm not going to be
            part of the world that you've created for me. And
            if I have to destroy the world you've created for
            me piece by piece so that I can create a new one,
            then that is what I am going to do.

            And this, Open Door, this is actually an act of
            destruction. A pacifist act of destruction. It's
            refusing to be afraid in the world you've created.
            And it is absolutely necessary, it is absolutely
            necessary because one day

one day when it's too late

one day they will say that this was human nature.

Helicopter in.

Helicopter overhead.

Helicopter out.

Pause.

Enter CHLOE.

CHLOE   62.

62 and counting. I'm just saying /

EMMA   Alright alright alright alright! For god's sake
Chloe!

CHLOE   I was literally just /

EMMA   Yes alright! All-right.

Pause.

CHLOE   W-ow.

It's like, totally deathly in here. What have you
guys been /

BILL   We have been having a reasonable discussion.

CHLOE   Oh

fuck.

She laughs.

BILL   Don't swear, sweetheart.

CHLOE   Of course you've been having a reasonable
discussion. That's why it feels like a fucking
bomb's gone off in /

BILL   I said, don't swear /

CHLOE   Like, bombs are the new reason for you people.
(*Laughs.*) Fuck me /

BILL   I said don't swear! /

CHLOE   Stop silencing me!

BILL   Christ.

         Pause.

CHLOE   I'm with Immy. Just so you know. I think we should let people in.

BILL   Yes, we know that. We do know that, and we're very proud of /

CHLOE   Don't patronise me.

BILL   Christ.

         Silence.

IMOGEN   So what are we going to do? It's up to you to decide what we're going to do. So.

         What are we going to /

CHLOE   I want to go outside.

EMMA   You what, darling?

CHLOE   I want to go outside. I want to go outside and /

EMMA   Stop it. Stop this immediately. Bill, stop her saying this /

CHLOE   I need to /

BILL   Don't be stupid.

CHLOE   I need to go outside and /

BILL   What? And what?

CHLOE   I need to /

EMMA   Help? You want to help?

BILL   She wants to go outside and help. Christ alive.

EMMA   Are you a paramedic?

CHLOE   No I /

EMMA	Because I didn't know that you were a paramedic. Or that you even have basic first-aid training /
CHLOE	I'm not a /
EMMA	Are you a police officer now? Is that what you are?
CHLOE	No I /
EMMA	Do you have military training? Are you part of a bomb-disposal squad?
CHLOE	No I don't, you know I /
EMMA	So what do you think you're going to do! Start an A-level revision group in the middle of the street? In the middle of the in the middle of a /
CHLOE	I don't want to go to help.
	I want to go to see.
EMMA	To see?
CHLOE	I want to
	I want to see. I need to see. I need to feel –
	It's not the same on the television. It makes it fake and it has to be real. I need to /
EMMA	You need to
	she needs to see.
CHLOE	I do. I need to /
EMMA	No. That is not
	this is not –
	No. No Chloe.
	We did not bring you up. We did not bring you up to –
	This is not an exhibition. This is real. It is not a not a

this is not a video game or a or some reality TV /

CHLOE   I didn't say that. I didn't say that, it's actually
because of that, that's exactly why I need to /

EMMA   No no no no no. It's like the executions all over
again /

CHLOE   No it's not! It's not like –

Actually it is like. Yes. That's why. It's the same
thing. I need to. I need to see and

feel. I really need to. I need to see this stuff. I need
it to be real. Because there's all this stuff that just
happens and we're not connected to it and I need
to be –

I need it to be real.

And you need to understand my needs /

BILL   I will lock you in your room.

I will lock you in your room. I am not joking.
Chloe. For your own good. I will lock you in
your room.

Listen to me.

Sweetheart.

Look at me.

If you try to leave this house tonight, I will lock
you in your room. And I will sit outside the door
all night if I have to.

You will not leave this house to –

None of you. Emma, you too. Emma this includes
you.

No one will leave this house tonight. Not tonight.
I will barricade the doors and windows. I will
barricade the doors and windows and stand there
with a kitchen knife rather than have any of you
leave this house tonight.

No one is going to leave this house until it is safe.
Until the government

until the government has told us it is safe.

Not to see. Not to help. Not to anything.

Do you understand?

Does everybody understand?

EMMA   (*Soft*.) Oh my god.

          Silence.

IMOGEN   Someone wants to come in.

          Pause.

          I said someone wants to come in. They're nearby.
          They've run away from the

          incident.

          They were there. They're scared. They want to

          they want to come in.

          They want our address.

          So I think what's going to happen now is that you
          need to make a decision. You need to make a
          decision quickly.

          And I need you to think, I need you to think when
          you're making your decision, that it could be
          Elizabeth. It could be your niece. My cousin.

          My. Cousin.

          Right now, asking someone for help. Asking a
          family like us for help. Because she's out there too
          and we don't know where she is but maybe
          somewhere

someone

a family like us will be giving her a home just like this one. Just for the night.

I really need you to think about that.

And then you can tell me whether I can give him our address.

EMMA   Him.

Give Him our address.

Why did it have to be a man?

Blackout.

Scene Two

Lights up.

BILL *and* EMMA.

Off, television on.

Silence.

BILL   I love you.

EMMA   What?

BILL   I said I love you.

I think it's important to say it, particularly at times like /

EMMA   Yes yes.

BILL   Right. So

              I love you. I have loved you to the point of
              anxiety. And I love our daughters. And I love you
              most of all.

EMMA   Thank you.

BILL   I think it's important to remind ourselves /

EMMA   Of course /

BILL   I think it's important to remind each other.

EMMA   Well I love you too.

BILL   Thanks.

              Silence.

EMMA   We made the right decision /

BILL   I know we did /

EMMA   It was the only decision we could have made /

BILL   Of course it was.

              We are

              good people.

EMMA   Yes.

BILL   And it is important to us to be /

EMMA   Good people. In the world. Yes.

              Better people, at least. Better than some /

BILL   Better than others /

EMMA   Yes.

              Pause.

BILL   You're scared.

EMMA   I am not scared /

BILL   You are scared. That's alright, you can be /

EMMA   I am not allowed to be scared. I haven't been
            scared since the day Imogen was born.

BILL   Well I've been nothing but scared since the day
            Imogen was born. So.

            Silence.

EMMA   Fuck.

            Birds.

BILL   Birds?

EMMA   I used to be scared of birds, you remember?

BILL   Oh yes.

EMMA   It's a phobia.

BILL   Exactly.

EMMA   And one day, you remember, on maternity leave
            for Chloe and Imogen must have been four. And
            that bird got into the house. A magpie. A huge
            bird. Imogen wasn't afraid at all but she didn't
            know what to do so she called me and –

            Flapping about. Smashing into. Feathers, blood
            and shit everywhere.

            I thought I was going to die but I had to pretend.

            Come here bird. Come here silly bird. It's alright
            darling, it's just a silly bird. It's just a bird it's just
            a bird it's just a bird.

            But she saw. She's not stupid. She knew.

            Pause.

BILL   I worry about Imogen. It's like she hasn't grown
            up or –

            Walks around the place with these huge eyes /

EMMA   Maybe that's what you want.

BILL   That's not fair /

EMMA   Your little girl /

BILL   No that's not fair. And it's not true. It's just

            their naivety. It's

            mind-blowing.

EMMA   Right. We were idealistic but /

BILL   Not naive.

EMMA   You couldn't be naive. Growing up thinking the
            whole world could come to an end any second /

BILL   Exactly.

EMMA   Are. Are idealistic.

BILL   Of course! Are idealistic. Just

            realistic now too.

            Helicopter in.

            Helicopter overhead.

            Helicopter out.

            Enter CHLOE, *TV room.*

CHLOE   Literally fuck these fucking helicopters and it's
            82. Just in case you're wondering.

            82.

            And no, I haven't heard from Elizabeth.

            Exit CHLOE, *TV room.*

BILL   I wish she'd stop doing that. It's like she's
accusing us. As though it's our fault or /

EMMA   Maybe it is.

BILL   No.

No. We don't start to think like that. We've done
our

best. We've always done our best to –

We are not actively –

You know.

EMMA   I need Elizabeth to be safe.

BILL   She will be safe. She is safe. I'm sure she's safe.

But there. Well there

there you can see

in terms of fault I mean. Her parents, your sister /

EMMA   I know I know /

BILL   Their attitudes, their beliefs. They are /

EMMA   Don't, it's embarrassing. It'll just make me angry /

BILL   Well it should. It should make you angry. They are
actively contributing to this kind of a world, with
their –

The way she talks about immigrants, about
refugees /

EMMA   She doesn't know the difference /

BILL   Anyone foreign. Anyone –

'I'm not racist but', she actually says things like
that /

EMMA   And now /

BILL   Now.

            Now look.

EMMA   Not that she'd recognise that it's partly her /

BILL   Oh no. Things like this just add fuel to their fire.

            People like that.

            And we're not like that.

EMMA   No.

BILL   We've never been like that.

EMMA   But sometimes I'd like to get all of the people like
            them and all the terrorists and just put them on an
            island somewhere so they can exterminate each
            other.

            Pause.

BILL   I will protect you.

            You and our daughters. Anything that –

            I will protect you.

EMMA   Will you? (*Laughs.*)

            Is that so? (*Laughs.*)

            Pause.

            When this is over, I'm going to fuck you like
            you've never been fucked before.

            Just to show we're still alive.

            He moves to her

            a knock on the door

            a high note

            they freeze

more knocking

enter IMOGEN *and* CHLOE

stop

BILL   Well Imogen. It's your big moment.

knocking, frantic

IMOGEN *frozen*

CHLOE   Go!

IMOGEN *to the hallway*

she goes down the hallway

she opens the door

she is there in the doorway with him in front of her and through the open door we can hear

distant but not too distant

helicopters sirens shouting burning

chaos

he steps into the hallway

she steps back into the hallway

he closes the door behind him and it is quiet again

she backs up down on the hallway

he walks down the hallway

she steps into the room

Enter JOHN.

He is wearing a coat and has a backpack. He is dusty, dishevelled.

He is different to them.

He is British Asian.

He is not what they expected and he is not necessarily what they want.

He stands.

He breathes.

Silence. Long.

IMOGEN   So this

this is John, everyone /

Explosion of greetings.

BILL   (*At once.*) Hello hello come in /

EMMA   (*At once.*) Welcome, John, please come in /

CHLOE   (*At once.*) Hi! Hi hi hi /

JOHN   Hi.

BILL   Right. Well. Bill. Hello.

BILL *extends his hand. He shakes* JOHN*'s hand.*

Gosh you're quite dusty.

JOHN   I'm sorry /

BILL   No no! No no no that wasn't what I meant at all. Not at all.

My wife, Emma /

EMMA   Hello, welcome.

JOHN   Hello Emma. Thank you.

BILL   And Imogen and Chloe /

CHLOE   Hi.

JOHN   Hi. Chloe.

BILL   I suppose you already know Imogen. Or know in
            a sort of modern sense of the word...

JOHN   Thank you for welcoming me into your home.

            Explosion of protestations.

BILL   (*At once.*) Our home is your home /

CHLOE   (*At once.*) Oh my god seriously /

EMMA   (*At once.*) Not at all! Please

            please make yourself comfortable. Please sit
            down. Can I take your coat? Bill, take his /

JOHN   No thank you.

EMMA   Are you sure? It's quite warm.

JOHN   I'm cold.

BILL   The shock, I expect /

EMMA   Oh of course, the shock!

BILL   We can turn the heating up /

EMMA   That's right! We can turn the

            would you like us to turn the

            Bill, turn up the /

JOHN   No, no thank you.

EMMA   I hate for you to be uncomfortable.

JOHN   I'm not uncomfortable. You're very kind.

EMMA   Well as long as he's not uncomfortable.

            Pause.

            Would you

            like something to eat?

JOHN   No thanks /

EMMA   Are you sure? There's plenty /

BILL   Or a drink, I expect you need a drink /

JOHN   No, really.

            Pause.

            Or maybe. A glass of water? If I could /

EMMA   Of course! Water. Imogen.

            Exit IMOGEN, *kitchen.*

            JOHN *is sitting.*

            They stare at him.

            A tap runs.

            A tap stops running.

            Enter IMOGEN *with a glass of water.*

            She gives it to JOHN.

            He drains the glass.

            Silence.

CHLOE   What's it like outside?

EMMA   Chloe!

CHLOE   What?

EMMA   I'm so sorry John /

CHLOE   What!

EMMA   Chloe that is clearly not appropriate /

JOHN   Hell.

            It is

            like hell.

            Pause.

EMMA   My god.

            Silence.

CHLOE   Did you see any dead people /

EMMA	Chloe. Your room. Now.
CHLOE	But /
EMMA	I said your room /
CHLOE	You can't /
BILL	She's overexcited /
CHLOE	That's so patronising!
BILL	Don't you dare /
CHLOE	And it's actually really sexist /
JOHN	Lots of dead people.

> And people that aren't people any more. Just bodies
>
> unconstructed.

BILL	I know you're in shock John but they're very young and /
CHLOE	We are not young!
BILL	Yes you are!
CHLOE	In some countries I'd be married with children by now /
BILL	Oh, well in some countries –

Pause.

| JOHN | Can I please have another glass of water? |
| CHLOE | I'll get it. |

Exit CHLOE, *kitchen.*

A tap runs.

A tap stops running.

Enter CHLOE *with water.*

JOHN *drains the glass.*

EMMA   Thirsty boy…

JOHN   Yes.

            Pause.

EMMA   You're safe now.

            John?

JOHN   Thank you.

EMMA   There's no need to be scared.

            You can relax. You can relax and –

            Would you like to take your coat off?

JOHN   I'm still cold.

BILL   The shock.

            Silence.

JOHN   Do you have /

            The family jump.

            Sorry

            but do you have any apples?

EMMA   Apples?

JOHN   I have a craving for apples /

BILL   An apple! Of course!

EMMA   But do we have any apples?

BILL   Of course we have apples! Everyone has apples /

EMMA   Only because I buy them, and I don't remember
            buying apples this week /

BILL   Well it's not like they go off /

            Exit IMOGEN, *kitchen.*

EMMA   Of course they go off!

BILL   Well of course ultimately they go off, everything
                   ultimately goes off /

EMMA   We just eat them before they go off /

BILL   Well of course we eat them before they /

EMMA   And I'm just not convinced that we have /

CHLOE   Can you guys literally stop talking about apples /

BILL   Stop saying literally /

CHLOE   But you're being really weird /

                   enter IMOGEN *with an apple*

                   she goes to JOHN *and holds out the apple*

                   they look at each other

EMMA   We are not being weird, we are trying to ascertain
                   whether we have any /

CHLOE   John's going to think he's come into a house full
                   of crazy people /

BILL   I thought we weren't allowed to use the word
                   crazy /

CHLOE   I didn't mean it like that!

                   JOHN *takes the apple.*

BILL   Isn't that what you two call a double standard /

JOHN   And the woman gave to me and I did eat.

BILL   What was that, John?

JOHN   I said, and the woman gave to me and I did eat.

BILL   Why did you say that?

                   Pause.

JOHN   I don't know.

Maybe I am in shock...

EMMA   Of course you're in shock! He's in shock, Bill!

BILL   Of course he's in shock!

JOHN eats the apple.

The family watch.

JOHN   The apple

is a very good apple.

EMMA   Right. I think we should all just relax. We're all
going to relax now and /

CHLOE   I'm relaxed /

BILL   Chloe /

CHLOE   It's you that's not relaxed /

EMMA   Well now we're all going to be relaxed. We're
going to be relaxed and we're going to have a nice
conversation –

That is

John, would you like to have a conversation?

JOHN   Okay.

EMMA   Good. Let's all just have a conversation.

Pause.

So

where are you from, John?

JOHN   London.

EMMA   And

and where is your family from? John.

JOHN   London.

EMMA   Where

where in London are you from?

JOHN   West London.

EMMA   I am also from London.

JOHN   And where are your family from?

EMMA   Oh! England, we're all English, very boring /

BILL   Your mother's father was from Ireland /

EMMA   Oh yes that's right! My mother's father was from Ireland, but I've never been so I forget.

JOHN   It must be nice

to be able to forget where your grandparents are from.

Pause.

Are you

from this part of London?

EMMA   No. No no no, I'm /

CHLOE   I am. I was born here. Literally in this house.

JOHN   Were you?

CHLOE   Yeah. But not, I mean obviously not right here. I was born upstairs. Not in the dining room.

JOHN   No. I don't expect you were born in the dining room.

The family laugh, not IMOGEN.

It dies.

EMMA   And. And what do you do, John?

JOHN   I'm doing a PhD.

BILL   Excellent. And what is your field of...?

JOHN   Mechanical engineering.

            Robots.

EMMA   Robots?

JOHN   By way of explanation, people don't always /

CHLOE   Do you actually make robots?

JOHN   Amongst other things.

CHLOE   Have you ever made a robot?

JOHN   Yes.

CHLOE   What does it do?

JOHN   Which one?

CHLOE   Any one.

JOHN   One of the robots picks up a marble in one place, carries it along a preset curve, and then deposits it in another place.

            Sorry to disappoint.

            Explosion of protestations.

EMMA   (*At once.*) No no! We didn't mean /

BILL   (*At once.*) No that's very interesting, really interesting /

CHLOE   (*At once.*) Oh my god I could literally never make a robot /

BILL	Spectacular!

Pause.

JOHN	Excuse me /
EMMA	(*At once.*) Yes /
BILL	(*At once.*) Yes /
JOHN	Can I use your bathroom? Please.
BILL	Of course!
EMMA	If you just, down the hall where you came in, on the left.
JOHN	Thank you.

Exit JOHN.

He takes his backpack with him.

Pause.

EMMA	He has impeccable manners.

I have no idea why I said that.

I've never said something so stupid in my /

CHLOE	He's quite cute.
EMMA	Chloe!
CHLOE	What?
EMMA	That is not appropriate /
CHLOE	I was just saying /
EMMA	Please don't say that /
CHLOE	But I was just /
EMMA	You'll upset your father /
BILL	Upset me?
EMMA	Don't say that again.

Pause.

BILL   He's a bit on edge isn't he?

IMOGEN   I like him.

BILL   Well that's very good that you like him. We're
            glad that you like him, but I'm just pointing out
            that he's a bit on edge /

IMOGEN   Shall we stop talking about him now? Like he's
            not here /

CHLOE   Well he's not here, technically.

IMOGEN   It's making me uncomfortable /

EMMA   Yes alright Imogen /

IMOGEN   Talking about him like he's not a not a –

            It's making me uncomfortable.

EMMA   Yes, alright. Imogen.

            Pause.

IMOGEN   It's just rude /

BILL   We've invited him into our house, haven't we?

IMOGEN   That doesn't give us rights over him /

BILL   I didn't say that. I didn't say that. You're always
            twisting my /

            Enter JOHN.

JOHN   I'm feeling less on edge now.

            You have a lovely home.

EMMA   (*At once.*) Well thank you /

BILL   (*At once.*) Oh, this old place /

IMOGEN   Don't say that. We do have a lovely home. We're
            very lucky and we're very grateful /

EMMA   Yes alright, Imogen! /

JOHN   What's that?

            A sculpture.

CHLOE   That's mine. I made it.

JOHN   What is it?

CHLOE   It's. Well.

            It's art.

JOHN   Art?

            JOHN *goes to the art.*

CHLOE   Don't look at it, it's my GCSE final piece, it's
            really stupid /

JOHN   What does it mean?

            I thought modern art was supposed to mean
            something?

CHLOE   Oh! Well. It's. Well, I mean, like I say it's really
            stupid but –

JOHN   Yes?

CHLOE   Well you have to turn it on.

            JOHN *moves to turn it on.*

IMOGEN   No don't!

            JOHN *stops.*

            JOHN *turns it on.*

            Moving images. Refracted and distorted.

            CHLOE *switches off the lights.*

            Pause.

JOHN   This is

          execution footage.

CHLOE   Yeah.

JOHN   You are

          interested

          in executions?

CHLOE   More like

          screens. I'm interested in screens. And

          violence, I guess.

JOHN   And you made this? The structure?

CHLOE   Yeah.

JOHN   This is

          melted plastic. Warped into these forms.

CHLOE   Yeah. Yeah I like working with funny materials.

JOHN   I like working with funny materials too.

CHLOE   When you make robots?

JOHN   Amongst other things.

IMOGEN   Turn it off!

          He turns it off.

          Lights on.

JOHN   Sorry.

IMOGEN   No it's just –

          It's not your fault but

          I hate it.

CHLOE   Immy doesn't like looking at horrible things. But
           I think that's why you have to look at them,
           because they're horrible.

JOHN   And what do you do, Imogen, while you're not
           looking at horrible things?

IMOGEN   I'm studying too.

JOHN   What?

IMOGEN   I'm studying too.

JOHN   I meant, what are you studying /

IMOGEN   Oh! Stupid of me /

JOHN   No, I wasn't clear /

IMOGEN   No it was my fault. I'm doing Politics and Social
           Anthropology.

JOHN   And are you acquiring many transferable skills?

           A high note.

IMOGEN   Oh.

EMMA   Imogen?

IMOGEN   I need to /

EMMA   Imogen what's wrong?

IMOGEN   I need to /

EMMA   Sit down /

BILL   What did you do to her?

EMMA   Are you alright? Imogen are you alright?

IMOGEN   I need a drink I want a drink I just want a /

EMMA   Bill.

           BILL *pours* IMOGEN *wine.*

She drinks.

IMOGEN   I'm sorry. Something happened. But I'm okay now.

EMMA   Just take your time /

IMOGEN   Our cousin's missing.

EMMA   Imogen /

IMOGEN   She's missing, our cousin /

EMMA   Imogen, don't /

IMOGEN   She was out tonight, where it all happened. She was out with friends and

we haven't heard from her and she's not reading messages and we can't get through to her and no one can get through to her. Not her parents. Not us.

No one.

JOHN   I'm sorry.

IMOGEN   This is her /

EMMA   Imogen!

IMOGEN shows JOHN her phone.

IMOGEN   Did you see her? Did you –

He studies the photo.

JOHN   No. I'm sorry, but no. I didn't see her.

IMOGEN   Oh.

Pause.

JOHN   Perhaps someone is looking after her just as you're looking after me. Perhaps someone, a family just like you, has been kind and taken her in and given her a home just as you have with me. Just for tonight.

Perhaps.

Pulse.

Blackout.

Scene Three

Lights up.

JOHN, IMOGEN *and* CHLOE.

JOHN *has a row of two apple cores in front of him. He is peeling a third apple with a small knife, stripping the skin in a single spiral.*

Off, television on.

JOHN   They were saying that he shot the bouncers and went down into the club and detonated the bomb. I expect this is where many of the casualties have come from. I don't think many people could have survived that. And then the smoke, and the fire.

They were saying that the second bomb was at an outside space. He didn't get into the bar. There wouldn't have been as many casualties but it was still quite bad. Perhaps he panicked. I can imagine that one could panic.

This is what they were saying on the street.

There were men with guns. You could hear the gunfire. There were several points of attack, and several times of attack, so it was hard to know where to run to. There are so many bars and clubs in that area, any of them could be a target and it felt as though they had established some form of perimeter.

But perhaps it only felt like that.

I hid behind a car. There was a man behind th
A white man. He looked at me and was afraid.
moved as if to hurt me, and instantaneously there
was guilt in his eyes. I saw, in one eye, his fear of
me, and in the other eye his guilt at his own
response.

It's a funny condition, these days, the human
condition.

JOHN *passes* CHLOE *the spiral of apple skin. She
chews on it. An exchange that has developed.*

I met a girl on the street and she was holding her
phone as though she had forgotten what it was for.

There was blood on her face but I don't think it
was her own because she didn't seem to be hurt.
Then I saw that there was blood on her phone and
she must have put it to her face. I don't know how
she could have blood on her phone but not be
injured herself.

I have just thought that perhaps it wasn't her own
phone.

She said to me, I don't know whether to film or to
find out what is happening. She held the phone out
to me like it was an alien object.

She held the phone out and it bled.

Enter EMMA.

EMMA   93.

          Pause.

          Everyone okay in here?

CHLOE   Yeah.

EMMA   Are you okay, John?

JOHN   Yes thanks.

EMMA   You don't need anything?

JOHN   No, thanks.

EMMA   Well you just let us know.

You two need anything?

CHLOE   We're fine.

EMMA   Good.

I'm just going to try and have a rest, I think. But if you need anything…

Exit EMMA.

Pause.

JOHN   I have a friend, he's in the army. He was deployed in the last war. He told me that he was in a camp, a very big camp, waiting to be stationed elsewhere. The camp was attacked and they were watching it unfold on the news on their phones. They learnt what was happening to them right there and then by watching the news from thousands of miles away.

That's what it was like on the street.

We were there. But we were also not there because we didn't know where it was that we were.

It's not so far away from here, you can hear it when you walk in the street. I walked under the trees in this residential area and heard the gunfire.

I expect that's what it's like to live in a war zone. To walk home under the trees and hear the gunfire.

I expect you get used to it.

Silence.

CHLOE   Thank you.

JOHN   My pleasure.

CHLOE   No really. It's like

          I needed to know. You know?

JOHN   Are you going to make some art now?

IMOGEN   That's a terrible thing to say.

JOHN   What?

IMOGEN   That you might get used to it. That you just get used to living in a war zone or /

JOHN   Why?

IMOGEN   Because it's normalising trauma. And it's wrong to –

          I'm sorry but I just don't think that it's right. To say that.

JOHN   I think we can get used to anything. I think it's particularly amazing, what we can get used to. Sometimes I think it's stranger that we've got used to this way of living. Sometimes I think that that is very strange. Eating all the time, intoxicated all the time, television all the time.

          I don't think that we were meant to get used to this. And I wonder whether it is more normal for us to exist in a war zone.

IMOGEN   It isn't.

JOHN   Is that what your Social Anthropology studies tell you?

IMOGEN   Of course there are differing opinions in an academic field.

JOHN   Then it's right that you should choose the opinion that most aligns with your worldview.

          Pause.

CHLOE   Your friend in the army, what did he say it was like?

JOHN   Boring, mostly.

CHLOE   (*At once.*) Boring!

IMOGEN   (*At once.*) Boring!

JOHN   Mostly.

IMOGEN   That's a terrible thing to say. I don't think it was boring for the local people /

JOHN   I wouldn't know.

IMOGEN   Well it doesn't take much imagination to /

JOHN   You find a lot of things terrible.

          To say, that is.

          Enter BILL.

BILL   Everyone alright in here?

CHLOE   I said yes, Dad, yes!

BILL   Don't get angry /

CHLOE   I'm not angry!

          Pause.

BILL   It's 95.

          Just so you. If you wanted to –

          Emma's having a little rest. Just in there.

          Everything alright, John?

JOHN   Yes thanks.

BILL   What are you doing there?

JOHN   We're talking.

BILL   About what?

JOHN   Terrible things.

BILL   What?

CHLOE   (*At once*.) Stuff, Dad! Just stuff!

IMOGEN   (*At once*.) Leave us alone!

            Pause.

BILL   John. Help yourself to wine.

JOHN   Thank you.

            Exit BILL.

            JOHN *does not help himself to wine.*

CHLOE   So I've been thinking about this thing, right, and
            as an example, my ex, Freddie, he was really great
            in some ways, but /

IMOGEN   John doesn't want to hear about Freddie /

CHLOE   It's not actually about Freddie if you /

JOHN   I don't mind hearing about Freddie /

CHLOE   I said it's not about Freddie!

EMMA   (*Off, shout*.) They're just talking!

            JOHN *halves the apple.*

            He gives half to IMOGEN *and keeps the other
            half for himself.*

CHLOE   So anyway the point is, about Freddie, is that for
            example, he'd say he was a feminist and stuff but
            actually I don't think he was because when there

was food or something he'd always give himself
a bigger portion than me and I think that's
probably quite a male thing to do, I mean, hashtag
Not All Men, but I don't think most women would
do that and the fact is in the end I just didn't find
him sexually attractive because –

JOHN   Why didn't you find him sexually attractive?

CHLOE   Well

it was sort of like

there was nothing there. Like it looked like he
knew how to talk the talk and even walk the walk,
but I actually don't think he believed it, any of it,
and the thing is it's not his fault because we all
look like we know how to walk the walk and talk
the talk like, for example, my school's totally in to
Intersectionalism now because Immy came back
from university and was like

Intersectionalism

so I went into school and was like,

Guys, my feminism will be intersectional or it will
be bullshit

and everyone was like, Yeah, my feminism will
be intersectional or it will be bullshit but actually
I go to this private school and I swear there are
only like three black people there and that's not
very intersectional or at least diverse and then
recently my friend got into this argument with
one of the black girls about what
Intersectionalism is and afterwards I suddenly
thought that it might not be okay to argue with
a black girl about what Intersectionalism is if
you're white but I just don't know.

JOHN   I see.

CHLOE   And I don't mean to be too down on everything
           because it's still really amazing in some ways if
           you think that when Immy was at school there
           wasn't even any feminism at all, except for weird
           girls with no friends like Immy /

IMOGEN   Chloe!

CHLOE   But to get back to Freddie sometimes I just don't
           see the point in him existing.

JOHN   I see.

CHLOE   Because we had this argument where I was saying
           I could understand why these men do the bad
           things, I mean the terrorists and the ones that go to
           fight. Because actually their worlds have been
           destroyed, by us, it's true, and their homes and
           their families and everything and it's like, of
           course they want to fight! Wouldn't you want to
           fight? And even the ones from this country –

JOHN   Yes?

CHLOE   Well, I'm just saying, there's so much racism and
           stuff so of course they're angry and they want to do
           something, they want to fight, and I was telling
           Freddie I could understand that. I understand how
           they feel. And actually, if I were them, I'd fight too.

           And Freddie was like, No way, He would never,
           How could I even say that, and suddenly I just felt
           cold inside, and suddenly I found myself thinking,
           Well what would you do?

           Really?

           I mean who are you, what do you really believe?
           I don't believe you really believe in anything at
           all. And you're just walking around saying all the
           right stuff but inside. There's nothing there. Like
           he's just a

           I don't know.

Like an avatar.

And the cold inside was this chill of realising that
I'm fucking an avatar.

An avatar for...

What? A decent modern man?

But it's easy to be a decent modern man, isn't it?
Whereas it's much harder to actually

engage

or.

And it's like there's all this stuff happening and
I'm just here making Art for my A levels and
thinking about art school because that's just this
acceptable way for me to engage but actually if
I were them I would want to engage properly. Like
really engage. I would want to fight. And it scares
me but I think I actually would. And what scares
me most of all is I think there's a part of me now
that's trying to make this imaginative leap, to –

A part of me that's trying to imagine whether I
could go and fight all the same. I mean despite
everything. I mean –

That's all I'm trying to say.

What do you think?

What do you think, John?

John?

JOHN   I think they would think that there are things
         you're better suited to than fighting.

IMOGEN   How dare you say that to my sister.

JOHN   Sorry /

IMOGEN   No how dare you say that. You don't say that.

And who on earth is They anyway? It's just this language over and over again They They They I'm so sick of it I'm drowning in it.

I thought better of you.

Pause.

JOHN   Okay.

Say you went to fight. What kind of fighting would they have you do? Do you think? What kind of fighting would you be prepared to do?

Would you strap on a bomb?

Would you?

Or is that not your idea of fighting?

Not what you had in mind?

What exactly did you have in mind?

You imagined

a woman.

With a machine gun.

She is in a desert. She is standing on a rock.

She has belts of ammunition slung across her chest and her shoulders. Her shirt is open at the neck.

She is lean and muscular, but not unattractively so. In fact, she is beautiful.

And her long hair blows in the wind /

IMOGEN   (*Stands.*) I'm going to be sick /

BILL   (*Off, shout.*) Chloe!

CHLOE   (*Shout.*) Wha-at!

EMMA   (*Off, shout.*) Don't shout in the house!

BILL   (*Off, shout.*) Chloe come here a minute.

CHLOE   (*Shout.*) Why me?

EMMA   (*Off, shout.*) I said, don't shout in the house!

CHLOE   Don't say anything interesting while I'm gone.

           Exit CHLOE, *TV room.*

           Pause.

JOHN   Are you okay?

IMOGEN   Yes.

JOHN   I'm sorry if I /

IMOGEN   No I'm sorry.

           And I'm sorry about Chloe.

JOHN   Why?

IMOGEN   I mean, she's fine. She's actually a really nice person. But she sort of doesn't understand things. So sometimes she says stupid things.

JOHN   She reminds me of my little sister.

IMOGEN   Does she?

JOHN   I used to think my little sister didn't understand
              things. Eventually it occurred to me that I didn't
              understand my little sister.

              Pause.

IMOGEN   Do you have any others?

JOHN   Other...?

IMOGEN   Siblings.

JOHN   Four.

IMOGEN   Four!

JOHN   Four sisters.

              Pause.

              You are

              imagining a world with four Chloes.

              Pause.

IMOGEN   Do you like them?

JOHN   They

              finish each other's sentences.

IMOGEN   Do they?

JOHN   And my mother. She knows how to do it too.

              Sometimes I'm overwhelmed by them all sitting
              there, finishing each other's sentences.

              Pause.

              My youngest sister is in love.

IMOGEN   Is she?

JOHN   She's so in love she's angry all the time.

              They laugh, wonder.

              She's so in love she's unable to finish the
              sentences, she can't remember how. And I think
              that makes her angry.

IMOGEN   Are you?
JOHN   In love?

IMOGEN   Able to finish the sentences.

JOHN   I struggle to start sentences, let alone finish them.

           I don't usually talk very much.
IMOGEN   No. Me neither. Usually. Unless it's sort of
           academic stuff or…
           But otherwise I find people a bit hard to talk to.
JOHN   (*Gentle*.) 'Weird girls with no friends like Immy.'

IMOGEN   No. No I wasn't weird I –

           Actually yes I was. I guess I was.
           Am.
JOHN   Don't worry. I'm weird too.
IMOGEN   Are you?
JOHN   Don't you think so?

IMOGEN   I think you're…

           Articulate.

JOHN   Ar-Tic-U-Late.
           I've been dreaming of the day when a woman
           would tell me I'm Articulate.

IMOGEN   No I didn't mean –

           It's a good thing, I /

           Enter CHLOE.

CHLOE   You're so immature!

           Slams door.

IMOGEN   What did they want?

CHLOE   They wanted to know what we were talking about.

IMOGEN   Oh.

CHLOE   I told them John was teaching us how to make
           a bomb.

           Jokejokejokejokejokejokejokejoke!

IMOGEN   Chloe!

CHLOE   It was just a joke!

IMOGEN   It's not funny, it's not /

JOHN   I could.

           If you wanted.

CHLOE   What? Like actually?

JOHN   If you wanted.

           Pause.

CHLOE   Go on then.

           JOHN *takes his phone out.*

           CHLOE *goes to him.*

IMOGEN   Chloe stop it!

CHLOE   It's interesting /

IMOGEN	Please stop it!
CHLOE	I think it's interesting, I think it's important to –

Are you literally looking it up on Google?

JOHN	Yes.
CHLOE	He's literally looking it up on Google.
JOHN	He is.
CHLOE	He's literally typed, 'How do you make a bomb' into Google.
JOHN	Well what did you expect?

CHLOE	I /
JOHN	Where do you think people start?
CHLOE	I just thought that /
JOHN	Do you think they go to special bomb school?
CHLOE	No I /
JOHN	'For A level I took IT, Maths and Bomb-Making.'
CHLOE	No that's not /
JOHN	Do you think they do degrees in bomb-making?
IMOGEN	'I am applying for a degree in Joint Art History and Bomb-Making.'
CHLOE	Stop it!
JOHN	'Having completed my degree in Bomb-Making at the University of Cambridge, I am well equipped for this position in International Terrorism.'
CHLOE	I said stop it it's not funny!
JOHN	It is quite funny.
CHLOE	Well it's not!
IMOGEN	She hates being teased /
CHLOE	Fuck you!

Enter BILL.

BILL   What's going on in here?

            Pause.

CHLOE   We were talking about Freddie.

BILL   About Freddie?

            Very well. Just don't think I don't understand.
            Because I do.

            Pause.

            Have you heard from Elizabeth /

CHLOE   No.

BILL   No.

            Emma is waiting for your aunt to call. We've
            phoned a few times but –

            I just want you to know that we're in control of
            the situation and everything's fine.

            Helicopter in.

            Helicopter above.

            Helicopter out.

CHLOE   Do you think it's journalists or soldiers? The
            helicopters.

IMOGEN   What's the difference?

BILL   Don't be facetious.

            Pause.

IMOGEN   You're so unkind to me now. It's like since I started
            to think and my thoughts weren't the thoughts you
            wanted me to have, when my thoughts weren't your
            thoughts, you've been so unkind.

            Pause.

BILL   I have to admit I'm feeling a little helpless.

I should very much like to put my daughters to bed.

If they were children still, I could put them to bed and talk with my wife about what is happening outside and, I expect, cry a little, and together we would decide how to talk to our daughters in the morning. Talk to our daughters in the morning about what's happened tonight, how best to explain to them, how best to explain without making them afraid and without teaching them to hate.

But they are not children and I cannot put them to bed so I'm just going to have a drink. John, are you sure you wouldn't like a drink?

JOHN   No thanks.

BILL   Not a drinking man, are you?

JOHN   Not really.

BILL   Well each to his own, as they say. Though I increasingly doubt that notion as a sensible way to manage society. Girls, would you /

CHLOE   (*At once.*) We're not girls we're women!

IMOGEN   (*At once.*) We're not girls we're women!

BILL   I am under a lot of stress tonight. I am keeping it together. I am really keeping it together. So stop getting at me. Alright? You're all going to stop getting at me now. There's been enough getting at me of late, and enough getting at me tonight.

And now you're going to tell me if you would like a drink.

CHLOE   Okay.

IMOGEN   Yes please.

BILL   Good.

He pours drinks.

CHLOE   What's happening outside?

BILL   Well, they are trying to decide whether to storm
          the venue.

IMOGEN   They can't!

BILL   Well they might have to /

IMOGEN   But they'll detonate the bombs they'll /

JOHN   They'll detonate the bombs anyway.

BILL   Is that so John?

JOHN   I expect they're waiting for the soldiers to storm
          the venue so that they'll cause more casualties
          when they detonate the bombs.

BILL   Is that so, John?

JOHN   I would, if I were them. Wouldn't you?

BILL   I have no idea, John. I have no idea what I would
          do if I were them because I would never be them.

          Pause.

CHLOE   How many people?

BILL   Hostages?

          Based on ticket sales 423.

IMOGEN   That's

          no that's

          no we have to negotiate, we always have to
          negotiate /

BILL   Well of course we want to negotiate but
          sometimes it's not possible and we have to make
          difficult /

IMOGEN   I don't believe in your choices, I don't believe in your difficult choices /

BILL   Well you better start /

           Where are you going?

           JOHN *has stood up*.

JOHN   To get a glass of water.

           Would you like one?

CHLOE   I want them to storm the venue.

           I need something to happen. I need

           I need

           I want it to happen.

           I don't know why.

IMOGEN   I don't know who you are. Who are you? How can you say that? How can we be /

CHLOE   She's always been like this. It's fucking /

BILL   Don't swear /

IMOGEN   Who are you and where did you come from /

CHLOE   She lives in this weird world of her own making and when the real world doesn't match up she just gets upset /

IMOGEN   You're bloodthirsty /

CHLOE   And you're pathetic /

IMOGEN   Because 95 is not enough for you, it's not enough /

JOHN   It'll be a great deal more than 95 when they detonate the bombs in the venue.

IMOGEN   When. When they detonate the bombs.

           When.

           You know you kind of make me sick?

           The phone rings.

BILL   Stay here.

           Exit BILL, TV room.

           The phone ringing.

           CHLOE *runs to the TV room.*

           The phone stops ringing.

           Pause.

IMOGEN   I'm scared.

           A high note

           JOHN *crosses the room and puts his hand on her shoulder*

           as JOHN *crosses a scream from the TV room which fills the room and becomes its own creature*

           CHLOE *runs from the TV room*

           BILL *runs out after her*

           BILL *catches her and holds her*

           she breaks away and runs out to the hallway and up the stairs

           BILL *follows*

           IMOGEN *turns to* JOHN *and puts her hand on his chest. She runs her hand up his chest to his shoulder and she takes his arm and she stands*

           they dance

BILL *carrying* CHLOE *to her bedroom*

EMMA *is collapsed in the TV room*

JOHN *and* IMOGEN *make their way back to the chair and she sits down again*

JOHN *with his hand on her shoulder*

BILL *rocking* CHLOE *in her bedroom*

IMOGEN *and* JOHN *in the dining room*

his hand on her shoulder

she looks ahead

blackout.

End of Act One.

Interlude – In Darkness

A high note

house lights out

debris of high note

IMOGEN'S VOICE   I'm just trying to find a way to make the things real.

I'm trying

I'm trying to find ways to –

And it's difficult because I'm not sure I really understand the nature of

everything.

But I have a feeling.

I have

a feeling

that is very powerful. The feeling is something to do with what you could call

um

the Essential Goodness of Mankind or

the Indomitable Nature of the Human Spirit

or

maybe

Truth and Beauty and Justice.

I was taught about those things. I was taught to
value those things. I believe in

those things.

They are my things.

And I begin to think, I do begin to think that these
could be your things too.

Now that you've come across this city all the way
across this city to me right to me right

to me

that we might

share those things

together.

Now.

That I might not be so alone with those things.
So all alone in the world with those things.

So I need you to know that I'm just trying to find
a way to make them real in the world, to make
them real to just

make it real

and

so

the truth is

I think you'll see that now you've come to me you will find my arms open. And if you come into my arms you will find that they wrap warm around you and if I wrap warm around you then you will discover how close I can hold you though I seem small hold you closer and closer and never let you go never let you go until you're part of me until you just bleed into me until the defining lines between you and me are just –

Until you are me.

Until you wake up one fine day and find that you are just

like

me.

But I am careful to avoid the word Love.

ACT TWO

Scene One

Phone ringing, a long time.

Lights up.

A bomb has exploded in the house but JOHN *and the family seem unaware.*

JOHN *and* IMOGEN.

The phone stops ringing.

IMOGEN   I'm scared.

            JOHN *crosses to her and puts his hand on her shoulder*

            a scream from the television room, then:

EMMA   (*Off.*) William!

            CHLOE *runs out*

            BILL *too, he takes hold of her*

CHLOE   This is your fault, it's your fault!

            she pulls away, she runs upstairs

            BILL *sees* JOHN *and* IMOGEN, *flounders, follows* CHLOE

EMMA   (*Off.*) Oh no. Oh no oh no /

            the TV room door slams shut.

            Silence.

IMOGEN   Oh.

            Oh.

JOHN   I'm sorry. I am so sorry.

          Pause.

IMOGEN   She held her phone out to you.

JOHN   Who?

IMOGEN   Elizabeth.

          She said

          she said /

JOHN   It wasn't her.

IMOGEN   I saw it. She had blood on her face.

JOHN   It was someone else /

IMOGEN   She said, I don't know whether to film or find out
          what's happening.

          That's just like her.

          Pause.

JOHN   Can I get you something? Can I get you some
          water?

          He makes to move.

IMOGEN   Don't!

          Don't move.

          Don't go anywhere.

          Just

          here.

I need you to be here.

Pause.

What did she look like?

Pause.

She had blood on her face.

That's just like her.

No it isn't.

Pause.

JOHN   This is

it's a family situation now. I should go.

He makes to move.

IMOGEN   I said don't move!

Not at all. Don't move. Just don't move

at all.

Pause.

You should stay the night. It's not –

You're not safe. We're not, any of us, safe.

Yes. You should stay the night. We have a spare
room. We're very lucky. I'll tell my parents

you're staying the night. It's safe in here. You'll be
safe. We'll all be safe if we just

stay very very still. For a moment.

Silence.

I'm not angry.

Pause.

I'm not angry at all, actually.

You might think that I would be angry but I'm not.
You see, I've taught myself how to be not angry.
Anger is a kind of fear and fear is the worst thing
so I taught myself to be not afraid of anything. My
mother is afraid of birds. She pretends not to be
but she is. Can you imagine being afraid of birds?
I can't. I used to be afraid of the dark. I'm not
afraid of the dark any more. I'm not afraid of
anything. And so I'm not angry at anything either.

No. That's not right. I'm very angry. I'm angry all
the time. Sometimes I'm so angry I think my heart
will stop. I wake up in the morning and I'm not
sure if my heart is beating because I'm so angry.
I wake up in the morning some days and I think
I've had a heart attack on waking. I'm so angry
sometimes my eyes and my ears start to hiss and
I have to stand up and walk across the room and
put my hands to my head and say I'm So Angry
I'm So So Angry just to do something because
otherwise I think I'll let blood out somewhere on
someone and perhaps myself. That's how angry
I am. I'm furious. I'm furious at us. I'm furious at
the world we've created.

I think we should destroy it.

No. That's not right either. I'm a pacifist. I don't
think we should destroy anything ever. Even bad
things. I think we should hold bad things close and
never let them go until they realise how loved they
are and stop being bad.

Yes.

That's how it works.

I'm angry at us. We deserve everything we get.
No. That's not right. No one deserves anything.

No, that is right. Everything we get.

We made it.

The meaning of the word Aftermath is the crop that
follows the first harvest which you harvest again.
This is the aftermath of our harvest. We deserve
this. We are guilty of this. We should reap it up and
eat it up. And smile. And say, Yes thank you very
much for our aftermath. It is very delicious thank
you and then we should hold them close and never
let them go until they know how loved they are.
How very very loved. And never again. And never
ever again what we have done what we did and
always hold them close as close can be and always
close and always loved and always –

Yes.

That's how it's going to work.

Silence.

Talk to me.

I need you to talk to me. I need you to be here and
talk to me. I need you to /

JOHN   Your pacifism is a luxury.

Pause.

IMOGEN   Yes. I suppose it is.

JOHN   They would rape and murder you.

IMOGEN   Yes I suppose they would.

           Please don't.

           Silence.

           John.

JOHN   Yes.

IMOGEN   I'm sorry I said you make me sick.

JOHN   It's fine.

IMOGEN   But you don't make me sick /

JOHN   I said it's fine.

IMOGEN   But John you don't /

JOHN   Leave it.

IMOGEN   It's just I don't want you to go and /

JOHN   I'm right here.

           I promise.

           Carefully, IMOGEN *puts her hand on* JOHN*'s hand on her shoulder.*

           Silence.

           Enter EMMA.

           JOHN*'s hand on* IMOGEN*'s shoulder.*

> IMOGEN*'s hand on* JOHN*'s hand.*

EMMA   What's going on in here?

> IMOGEN *removes her hand from* JOHN*'s hand.*

JOHN   She was /

EMMA   What are you doing touching my daughter?

JOHN   She was upset /

EMMA   Imogen, come here now right now /

JOHN   I was just /

EMMA   You shut up, you don't say anything. Imogen come here now.

> IMOGEN *goes to* EMMA.

How dare you touch my daughter. What are you thinking? You think because we welcomed you into our house you can touch my daughter? That you can put your hands on my /

IMOGEN   John's going to stay the night.

He's going to stay the night because we have a spare room. So

he's going to stay the night.

EMMA   He's going to stay the /

IMOGEN   So you have to tell him, you need to tell him that he has to stay the night, because it's not safe. So he can't go.

You need to think about it, you need to really think about it and then that's what you need to do. Because it's the right thing to do.

Pause.

EMMA   She's right.

She is right, John. You should stay the night. We have a spare room.

IMOGEN   We're very lucky.

EMMA   I apologise for losing my temper, but I'm feeling a little fragile and /

The phone rings.

Fuck! Bill!

EMMA *to the TV room.*

Stops.

Don't go anywhere. Either of you. It's not safe.

Exit EMMA.

The phone stops ringing.

Pause.

IMOGEN   I'm sorry about what she said but you have to understand she didn't mean it like that. She's afraid of birds like I told you and one time when I was little a magpie got into the house and she thinks I don't remember it but I do and sometimes she gets confused.

JOHN   Your explanation for what just happened is that your mother thinks I am a magpie?

IMOGEN   Well it's not such a bad thing being a magpie after all. Did you know they're the only animals except for great apes that can recognise their own reflection in the mirror?

JOHN   Are you okay?

          Imogen?

IMOGEN   I'm just saying it's not such a bad thing and I don't
           want you to go because you might get hurt and it's
           safe here /

JOHN   Is it?

IMOGEN   It is it is I promise you nothing will happen to you
           as long as you're with me and it's just really
           important that we get this right because one day
           they'll say that this was human /

JOHN   Don't.

IMOGEN   We have to make this work.

           We're going to prove it to them.

           You'll see.

           BILL *in the hallway.*

BILL   (*Off.*) What the hell's going on down here?

           Enter BILL.

           He stands in the entrance of the hallway.

IMOGEN   John's going to stay the night.

BILL   John's going to /

IMOGEN   He's going to stay the night. Mummy agreed. It's
           decided.

BILL   Oh it's 'decided' is it /

IMOGEN   It's decided.

           Pause.

BILL   Well I suppose we do have a spare room /

JOHN   Do you?

BILL   And it's not safe outside.

The government will let us know when it's safe.

So he's going to stay the night. Good.

Good.

Good good.

Where's Emma?

IMOGEN   She's on the phone.

BILL   Why was she shouting?

JOHN   She mistook me for a magpie.

BILL   What?

JOHN   Nothing.

BILL   What did you say?

JOHN   It was just a joke.

IMOGEN   There's no such thing as just a /

BILL   I've had just about enough of this! I've got Chloe
          crying upstairs, your mother shouting down here,
          your cousin blown to bits in a

          in a

          in a

          in a.

          I'm sorry. I'm feeling a little fragile, I'm sure you
          understand.

          Time for another drink, I think.

          Imogen?

IMOGEN	Yes.
BILL	John?
JOHN	(*At once.*) No /
BILL	(*At once.*) 'No thank you.'

It was just a joke.

IMOGEN	There's no such thing as just a /
EMMA	(*Off, shout.*) This is not the time this is clearly not the / time!
BILL	Christ what now!

Exit BILL, *TV room.*

EMMA	(*Off, shout.*) Of all the times you could –

(*Off, shout.*) I am listening!

The door slams.

Pause.

IMOGEN	It's really not such a little thing, you know, to be able to recognise your own reflection in a mirror.
JOHN	I don't expect

that it is.

Pause.

IMOGEN	John?
JOHN	Yes?
IMOGEN	Why are you here?

JOHN	Because you won't let me go.

IMOGEN	No, I mean

why are you *here*?

JOHN   I thought it was safer for me to be inside rather
              than outside, tonight.

IMOGEN   No, but. *Why are you here?*

JOHN   I packed my backpack and I put on my coat and
              I left the lab but I didn't go home. I started to
              walk. I walked until I came to the place with the
              bars and the restaurants and the people, all the
              drunk people finishing each other's sentences just
              like at home. It was already dark but the colours
              were so vivid. For a moment I had a sense that it
              was raining. And for a moment I had a sense that
              no one could see me and I stopped and stayed still
              and I waited for it all to pass by.

              Then

              there was the noise and

              everything was hot and

              burning.

              Pause.

              And you said, Come here, I will keep you safe.

              So now. I'm here.

IMOGEN   Why didn't you go home?

JOHN   I don't like it at home.

              It's noisy and I can't
              concentrate.

              And I don't like my family.

IMOGEN   Why don't you like your family?

JOHN   There are too many of them. And
they're all afraid.

IMOGEN   My family's afraid too.

JOHN   I know.

IMOGEN   Do you like my family?

JOHN   Not particularly.

IMOGEN   No. I don't think I like my family either.

JOHN   You're okay though.

IMOGEN   Thanks.

John?

JOHN   Yes?

IMOGEN   Are You afraid?

JOHN   No.

IMOGEN   Are you sure?

JOHN   Yes.

IMOGEN   Because I think I'm becoming afraid. And I'm
afraid of being afraid because it's sort of the worst
thing, isn't it? So if you're not then I /

JOHN   I'll stay if you want me to.

If that's what you want.

Is that what you want?

IMOGEN   That's what I –

            Yes.

JOHN   I'd like to then.

IMOGEN   Okay.

JOHN   See this

            spare room I've been hearing so much about.

IMOGEN   Thank you.

JOHN   For? /

IMOGEN   Staying with me.

JOHN   It's all a bit strange isn't it?

            Tonight.

            Pause.

IMOGEN   John /

CHLOE   (*Off.*) Right, I've been thinking about it, and I need
            you to hear me out here

            Enter CHLOE.

            but basically if someone has to die, which they do,
            then I suppose it may as well have been Elizabeth.

JOHN   I see.

            CHLOE *gets herself wine.*

CHLOE   No, you don't, but I'm going to explain.

Because she made this world, she helped make it
like this, she didn't do anything to make it better,
she actually made it

worse. So.

If somebody has to –

I mean she wasn't even a feminist! And she'd
actually say, like with pride, 'I'm not a feminist.'
I mean, what kind of person says that? And when
she didn't get into her top choice she blamed
positive discrimination, she was like, 'I'd totally
have got in if it weren't for all this unfair positive
discrimination' and it's like she can't even see that
she didn't get in because she doesn't know how to
think, like she actually doesn't know how to think.

And what kind of person our age is right-wing?
I mean seriously? How can you be our age and
actually be right-wing? Who does that? No really!
Literally who? And I guess you could say

I guess you could say it's not her fault because her
parents taught her that, they taught her to think
like that, to live like that but

the thing is

I find I keep saying things aren't people's fault.
Like it's not Freddie's fault he's an avatar, and it's
not Elizabeth's fault she's a small-minded racist
bigot, but actually, maybe if you're not strong
enough to get over that, to get over the fact that
it's not your fault and learn how to think in a not-
fucked-up fashion then –

I'm just saying.

JOHN   Why does someone have to die?

You said that someone has to die. So

why does someone have to die?

CHLOE   Because there isn't enough space.

There isn't enough space. There aren't enough resources. Do you know what animals do to each other if you don't give them enough space and enough resources?

Exactly what we're doing to each other.

A lot more people are going to die before we're through. A lot more. And here's the thing, I'd rather it was Elizabeth, and I love her, she's my cousin –

Was my cousin.

Pause.

But if it has to be someone, then it has to be her.

IMOGEN   Nobody deserves to die /

CHLOE   Actually you know what, Immy, I'm sorry but I think some people do. I decided tonight

to be honest about it from now on. And I think some people do.

JOHN   And what happens when they decide that you're the one who doesn't know how to think?

CHLOE   That's not how it works. I think the right things /

JOHN   Objectively?

CHLOE   Objectively. I think, objectively, the right things.

There are studies that show that I think the right things! There are theories, there are people, academics, philosophers, who know about these things and I think the things that they know.

JOHN   It's amazing. Your arrogance. It

is amazing.

Your arrogance, did you know that it's a death warrant?

CHLOE   Who the fuck's asking?

No really John, who the fuck's asking? I mean, who the fuck are you?

John? John?

John-nuh.

Actually who. In the fuck. Are /

JOHN   Stop it.

EMMA   (*Off.*) Well it's just incredible to me /

BILL   (*Off.*) It's inconceivable /

Enter BILL *and* EMMA.

EMMA   It is exactly that, inconceivable /

BILL   Well they're grieving /

EMMA   Of course they're grieving, I'm grieving, we're all grieving, everyone's grieving. But at a time like this /

BILL   To say those things at a time like this /

EMMA   Well it's just who she is /

BILL   Who they are, they can't help it /

EMMA   But I'm sick and tired of it, it's just small-minded, it's just a limited way of thinking /

CHLOE   What?

EMMA   Just your aunt. The things she says /

CHLOE   What things?

EMMA   You know what things, the usual things, things about people like him.

JOHN   What about people like me?

BILL   Put that down, you're too young to drink this much /

CHLOE   I'm going to be drunk tonight. Tonight and for the rest of my life. I'm going to be drunk for the rest of my life /

BILL   She's upset /

CHLOE   I am not upset. I'm actually not upset at all.

In fact, I'm feeling kind of exhilarated.

How do you feel about that? I think we should all talk about our feelings /

EMMA   John, you're still wearing your coat.

JOHN   Yes.

EMMA   Would you like us to take your coat now?

JOHN   No.

EMMA   He's still not warm, Bill.

BILL   Well I think it's perfectly warm /

JOHN   It's the shock. I expect.

BILL   You know what, I don't think he is in shock.

EMMA   You don't think he's in shock?

BILL   I see no evidence of him being in shock. Are you
            in shock, John?

JOHN   I don't

            know.

BILL   You see, he doesn't even know if he's in shock /

EMMA   Do people know if they're in shock?

BILL   Well I don't know, but if anything it seems to
            me as though he finds the whole situation pretty
            funny /

EMMA   Do you find the situation funny John?

JOHN   I don't find it funny /

BILL   It's a tragedy.

            It. Is a tragedy.

            Pause.

JOHN   It is a tragedy.

BILL   Well good. As long as we're all agreed on that
            then that's /

IMOGEN   I don't think it's a tragedy.

EMMA   You what, darling?

IMOGEN   I think it's an aftermath.

BILL   You /

EMMA   Don't ask her what she means by that, it'll only
            upset you /

JOHN   I expect we might all be in shock /

EMMA   And what would you know about it?

            Do you know anything about it?

Well do you?

JOHN   About what?

EMMA   Are you scared? Do you know what it feels like to be scared?

CHLOE   Obviously he knows what it feels like to be scared. Everyone's scared.

IMOGEN   I'm not scared.

EMMA   I'm just wondering, if it's alright, if it's not offensive for me to wonder something, I'm just wondering if John knows anything about

anything really.

IMOGEN   He knows about robots.

EMMA   Oh yes that's right he knows about robots /

BILL   Robots aren't scared.

JOHN   You can program a robot to be scared, if you want. You can program a robot to be

anything. You want.

BILL   Well it's not the same thing is it /

EMMA   Yes, it's not the same thing.

JOHN   I could make a robot for you that spoke and that would tell you it was scared. I could program it to respond to particular gestures and actions on your part and its response would be to say, 'I am scared.' I could program a robot to respond to everything you did and said with the response, 'I am scared.'

You're not a robot, but you're scared. So I wonder how much of that is programming, and how much of that is. Instinct.

BILL   I am not scared.

And even if I were, I'm not programmable.

JOHN   Of course.

BILL   Are you being sarcastic?

JOHN   No /

BILL   I won't have sarcasm in my house, not tonight /

CHLOE   Dad you're being embarrassing /

            BILL *smashes his wine glass on the floor.*

            BILL *takes* CHLOE*'s wine glass from her and*
            smashes that on the floor too.

BILL   There is only so much

            there is only so much that is acceptable.

            There is only so much –

            There is only so much.

            Silence.

JOHN   This reminds me of something I saw in a café
            quite recently. I was sitting at a high table and at
            the table next to me was a middle-aged woman
            and her, I assume, teenage daughter. I was aware
            of them talking in a very tentative and polite way,
            unable to say much to each other, which seemed a
            bit strange. There was something wrong with the
            picture and I couldn't work out what it was at first
            and then I realised, in an instant, that the girl was
            very severely anorexic.

            But very severely.

            She was entirely defined by her joints and sockets.
            And her head. And the rest of her was

            structurally inadequate. I could see on her arms in
            the light that came into the café, a film of pale fur.

She could only recently have been out of hospital, or perhaps only out for the day. I guessed that this must be an occasion for them both, and was quite touched by it. She was trying hard to eat, and her, I assume, mother was being very gentle and supportive.

Pause.

And then the, I assume, mother went to the bar to get a dessert for them to share. She was clear on this point, the sharing. I watched her come back from the bar with this amazing dessert: a large, pale-pink meringue, with a neon drizzle decoration, light puffs of cream and some strawberry halves. I was touched by that too, this extravagantly lovely dessert that this damaged mother and daughter were going to share together on their day out.

I watched her come back from the bar with the dessert on a plate and two tiny forks. She was almost back at her table, just two metres, approximately, from her, I assume, daughter, when suddenly

inexplicably

she dropped the whole thing, plate included. It smashed on the floor. Everyone stopped talking to watch and the daughter stood up to help, and then froze.

They both froze.

They both froze and stood in calamity staring at this huge fat sick spattered mess of cream and sweet and pink and china all mixed in spread between them and neither of them could do anything at all while everyone watched, while they both just stood there staring at all their fear and all their damage

visible now

between them.

And the mother kept saying, It's okay.

It's okay.

It's okay.

Everything is fine.

Everything is going to be just

fine.

Silence.

Helicopter in

JOHN *starts to laugh*

helicopter overhead

BILL   What's so funny?

JOHN   Sorry –

              he laughs harder

EMMA   Why is he laughing?

BILL   What's so funny, John? What's so funny about that story?

EMMA   It's a horrible story!

JOHN   It's not that. I must be in shock, traumatised even –

              he laughs

EMMA   Well I don't think this is funny at all.

CHLOE   Why are you laughing!

IMOGEN   Stop John stop!

              helicopter out

              he giggles

              he controls himself

JOHN   No, but in all seriousness, you really are good people, aren't you?

he giggles

All of you.

You really are just very good people. The best of people.

It's a pleasure, really, it is a pleasure, to have spent my evening with you.

pulse.

Blackout.

Scene Two

Lights up.

EMMA, CHLOE *and* IMOGEN.

The girls tucked under EMMA*'s arms on the sofa.*

The wine and broken glass uncleared.

Off, television on.

Silence.

CHLOE   What are they doing?

EMMA   I don't know.

Pause.

CHLOE   I want to go outside.

EMMA   You can't. It's not safe.

CHLOE   They're allowed outside.

EMMA   I know.

And we're going to sit here.

Pause.

It's so nice to cuddle you both.

So so nice.

Silence.

CHLOE   What are they doing?

EMMA   I don't know.

CHLOE   Why are they taking so long?

EMMA   I don't know.

CHLOE   I want to go into the garden too.

EMMA   We're not allowed. We're just going to sit here.

CHLOE   It's my garden /

EMMA   It is not your garden. It is my garden. And your father's garden.

          Silence.

CHLOE   I hate him.

EMMA   That's unkind and untrue.

          He loves you.

CHLOE   No not Dad. Dad's just kind of silly.

          I hate John.

          Pause.

EMMA   Yes.

          I think I hate John too. Though I don't for the life of me know why.

CHLOE   I wouldn't fuck him if he paid me.

EMMA   Well that's

          very good. I'm glad you wouldn't fuck him if he paid you.

CHLOE   Immy?

IMOGEN   What?

Oh! No. No I wouldn't fuck him. I mean, not if he paid me.

No.

Of course there's an argument that all fucking should be paid for. But I can't really remember how to make that argument any more.

You know, I think I might be a romantic, at heart. That despite myself and various theories I've tried to put into practice, I believe in love and intimacy and the necessary human wonder of two human people finding each other and creating a sexual and social world together.

Do you think that's problematic?

EMMA   No I think that's good.

Just be sure to protect yourself.

IMOGEN   From what?

EMMA   From the danger.

IMOGEN   What danger?

EMMA   The ones that kill.

Pause.

I'm afraid he's going to kill us.

CHLOE   What, like murder us? Like actually?

EMMA   No, not like that. Don't be stupid.

           Pause.

           I'm afraid he already has.

           I think we may have made a mistake. Letting the
           night in tonight. Letting whatever happened
           outside

           in. I think we may have made

           a mistake.

           Pause.

CHLOE   I don't.

           I've never felt so alive.

           I think this is the first time since I was a child that
           I've actually felt like I'm actually alive.

IMOGEN   You are terrifying.

           And you are wrong.

           And so are you.

           You're both just

           wrong. And it's amazing to me

           it's amazing to me how wrong you can be. How
           you can't see clearly. How none of you can see –

           How you can't see what I can see.

           And what he can see

           too.

EMMA   Well I just wouldn't be so sure about that if I were
          you.

IMOGEN   What?

EMMA   Just that /

IMOGEN   What.

EMMA   That /

IMOGEN   What.

EMMA   Just that it's important to remember that people
          are /

IMOGEN   What. What.

EMMA   Different.

IMOGEN   Different.

EMMA   People are /

IMOGEN   Different.

EMMA   That is not a /

IMOGEN   Dirty word.

          Okay.

EMMA   It's a form of respect. It's a form of respect to /

IMOGEN   Okay.

          Pause.

EMMA   When you were born –

          When you were born /

IMOGEN   This is irrelevant /

EMMA   Not to me.

           When you were born, when you first opened your
           eyes, you looked right at me. Right at me and /

CHLOE   Babies don't /

EMMA   She looked right at me. I know. I'm her mother,
           and your mother too, and I know.

           She looked right at me. And I looked back at her,
           and I had never loved like that. I knew that I loved
           you so

           much, and that it was absolutely impossible, the
           responsibility of loving so much. In this world, the
           responsibility of loving that much was
           completely –

           I love you both so much.

           And so I just want you to be safe. That's all that
           your father and I want. That's all that anyone
           wants, in the end, because that's

           just. How it works.

           And I'm sorry if you don't like that Imogen, and
           I'm sorry if you don't agree with that right now
           but you will learn that there are some things in life
           worth being afraid of, and that you will do
           anything, in the end, anything to keep the people
           you love safe. To keep

           the danger

           far away.

IMOGEN   Well I want everyone to be safe.

           Everyone.

           So that's what I'm going to do. And that's /

BILL and JOHN *in the kitchen.*

BILL   (*Off.*) Well it's really remarkable, I'd say it's really
            remarkable.

JOHN   (*Off.*) Yes.

BILL   (*Off.*) I've never heard anything like it.

JOHN   (*Off.*) No.

            Enter JOHN *and* BILL, BILL *wearing a coat now.*

BILL   It's incredible, in fact. To hear that. I expect that's
            what it's like to live in a war zone /

CHLOE   What?

BILL   The helicopters. The sirens. The shouting. The
            megaphones /

JOHN   The burning.

BILL   The burning?

JOHN   Couldn't you hear the burning?

BILL   The burning what?

JOHN   Just

            burning.

            Maybe a

            way of life. A way of living.

            Everything we thought we knew.

            Pause.

BILL   It makes me very uncomfortable when you say
            things like that. You've been making me
            uncomfortable all evening.

JOHN   I know.

BILL   Well at least he's calmed down a bit.

EMMA   Has he?

BILL   You've calmed down, haven't you John?

JOHN   I guess so.

           Actually I'm tired.

           Really so tired.

           Pause.

           It'll be over soon anyway.

           All of this.

IMOGEN   Why?

JOHN   Because they're going to storm the venue.

IMOGEN   No.

           They are going to negotiate.

           They are going to successfully –

           Pause.

           Do you think it's always like this? Negotiating?

           Just

           shouting into the dark like some kind of an idiot.

           It's disheartening.

           It's disheartening that no idiot shouts back.

           Silence.

EMMA   Bill take your coat off, you'll get hot.

BILL   Yes yes.

           BILL *takes off his coat.*

EMMA John?

JOHN No thanks.

CHLOE Why won't he take his coat off?

   I want to know, I need to –

   Tell him to take his coat off.

BILL (*Stepping forward.*) Let me take your coat, John.

JOHN (*Stepping back.*) No thank you.

EMMA Why? Why won't you take your coat off?

JOHN I don't want to be cold.

EMMA It's perfectly warm /

BILL Why won't you drink?

JOHN I don't want to be drunk.

BILL Well I've had just about enough of this, coming in here and not drinking /

EMMA And not taking his coat off /

BILL And just being John.

CHLOE If that is even his name.

JOHN Help me.

BILL Don't look at her, she's just a child /

JOHN Imogen.

IMOGEN I wish you could all just behave how I want you to behave. I've been trying all night. I've been trying so hard and none of you –

You just won't behave how I want you to behave.
How I dreamed you could behave. How we could
all –

And I don't know what to do with what you're
giving me and I'm trying and trying and trying and

trying

because all I've ever wanted is to be bigger than
everything that's around me and better and kinder
than everything that's around me but you're not
helping me, you're all just

crushing me, it's like everything is crushing me
and it's so disappointing it's so

disappointing

and

I'm sorry that I'm not big enough but how am
I supposed to be if everything's just designed to
crush me and /

BILL   Now look, you've upset her /

IMOGEN screams. Sharp.

Pause. Sharp. Bated.

JOHN   I'm going now.

He collects his backpack.

EMMA   (*At once.*) Go where? /

CHLOE   (*At once.*) Don't let him go!

BILL bars the hallway.

JOHN   Excuse me. I need to get past please.

Excuse me.

Excuse me.

Move. Now. Please.

CHLOE   Take off your coat.

JOHN   No.

CHLOE   Take it off!

JOHN   No.

BILL   Why won't you take your coat off, John?

JOHN   I don't want to take my coat off /

EMMA   I think you need to take your coat off. It's very warm and you're not in shock any more /

BILL   Just take your coat off. That's all we're asking.

JOHN   I don't want to take my coat off /

EMMA   It's not unreasonable to ask you to take your coat off. Do you think it's unreasonable, Bill?

BILL   Not at all. It's the least he could do /

EMMA   I think it's very rude of you to come into our home and not take your coat off /

BILL   Emma's right, it's just rude /

JOHN   I will not take my coat off.

Get out of my way.

CHLOE   What are you hiding under your coat? What are you –

What are you hiding /

EMMA   Just take off your coat!

JOHN   I will not take my coat off /

BILL   You're not leaving here until you've taken your coat off and shown us –

JOHN   Yes?

BILL   Shown us that you're not hiding anything under
            your coat.

JOHN   I see.

            I see /

IMOGEN   John.

            Please just –

            John.

            JOHN *looks at* IMOGEN.

            IMOGEN *doesn't look at* JOHN.

            JOHN *leaps to push past* BILL. BILL *moves*

            they collide

            EMMA *and* CHLOE *screaming*

            IMOGEN *watching*

EMMA   Get it off him! Get it off him! Get it off him! Get it
            off him! Get it off him! Get it off him! Get it off
            him! Get it off him! Get it off him! Get it off him!
            Get it off him! Get it off him! Get it off him! Get it
            off him! Get it off him! Get it off him! Get it off
            him! Get it off him! Get it off him! Get it off him!
            Get it off him! Get it off him! Get it off him! Get it
            off him! Get it off him! Get it off him! Get it off
            him! Get it off him! Get it off him! Get it off him!

            BILL *and* JOHN *struggle together*

            BILL *trying to take off* JOHN's *coat*

            JOHN *is younger and stronger. He begins to
            subdue* BILL

            CHLOE *helps* BILL

they all struggle on the floor

EMMA *kicking* JOHN

IMOGEN *watching*

JOHN *screams*

IMOGEN *off to the TV room*

they hold JOHN *down and pull off his coat*

EMMA *is left standing with the coat*

CHLOE *and* BILL *pull back*

JOHN *stands. He is wearing a top of some description*

his face bloodied

he breathes

silence

debris

EMMA   Well there we are.

         Pause.

         Here we all are then.

         Silence.

JOHN   You bit

         my face.

         You bit. My face.

CHLOE   I'm sorry /

BILL   She's in shock she's overexcited /

CHLOE   It's true. I actually am overexcited /

JOHN   There is only so much

          there is only so much that is acceptable /

BILL   No

          oh no oh no /

JOHN   There is only so much

          there is only. So. Much.

          Pause.

          Can I have my coat back now.

EMMA   Oh! Yes, yes of course.

          EMMA *gives* JOHN *his coat.*

          He puts it on.

          Right. Right.

          Now we are all going to /

BILL   Calm down /

EMMA   That's right. We're going to calm down and have a /

BILL   Reasonable discussion.

EMMA   Right. We're going to have a reasonable discussion –

          That is

          would you like to have a reasonable discussion, John?

          John? Would you like to have a reasonable /

JOHN   I am going to have a drink. And then I'm going to go.

He goes to the table and pours himself wine and stands and drinks the wine.

They watch him drink the wine.

Then:

CHLOE   We made a mistake.

We were asking the wrong question.

Don't you see?

She laughs.

John, what do you have in your backpack?

JOHN *stops drinking the wine.*

What do you have –

I need to know, I need to see

we need to /

JOHN   Be careful.

This time I will hurt you.

I will hurt you like you have never been hurt before.

Pause. Bated.

Can you hear it?

Distant, but not too distant, an explosion.

Enter IMOGEN.

IMOGEN   520.

520. I said.

Did you hear me?

The family rush to the TV room.

CHLOE   (*At once*.) We'll miss it /

EMMA   (*At once*.) William!

           IMOGEN *shuts the door behind them.*

IMOGEN   It might be more than that. I'm just guessing. Or
           maybe it's less. I don't really know. I added the
           ticket sales to the most recent count but obviously
           no one really knows exactly because everything's
           so confused now.

           Maybe we won't know for days.

           Maybe we won't ever –

           JOHN *turns to her.*

           A high note.

           Your face

           your face is bleeding.

           You have blood on your face.

           Hold your

           hand out to me.

           Hold your hand out to me like it was outside on
           the street and I swear to you I'll take it /

JOHN   You weren't there.

           Not on the street and not in here.

           And I was afraid.

           Because I am afraid.

           I'm afraid of everything.

I'm so afraid I don't even know how to breathe
any more. I don't even know how to think. I'm so
afraid of everything that I can't feel

anything.

Because if I start to feel then I'll feel too much
and it will kill me. It

will kill me.

And I needed you and you weren't there.

Pause.

IMOGEN   I'm sorry. John. I'm sorry. John I'm –

It's just

I'm a pacifist. I cannot engage in violent action of
any kind so there was nothing I could –

I could have put my body between your body and
their bodies and just lain still just lain heavy
between you

lain heavy against you.

I thought of that, I did think of that but /

JOHN   But?

IMOGEN   I was shy.

JOHN   You were shy.

IMOGEN   I was shy.

*JOHN is facing out and away from her. He is
silent.*

But his face moves with pain.

I think you're

I think you're the most beautiful thing I've –

I think you're –

I don't even know what to do with my thoughts or my hands I'm

I'm so scared of you it's like the language I learnt the language I learnt has

unfolded

or –

And I thought to myself that perhaps we could make a space together, you and I. That maybe before we turn bad like everyone else, before we go wrong like everyone else perhaps if we could go somewhere and make a space to

to make a different world or –

Because this one's done now. It's just done now. We ruined it and

if you and I could create another one I think that I believe that maybe we could –

Because it can't be that hard, can it? John? It can't be that hard to create a world, really. Can it?

John?

And it would work, I promise John that I could make it work and /

JOHN *gathers and controls himself*

Where are you going?

he collects his backpack

No please don't go no please don't it's not safe it's not –

he looks at her

he chatters like a magpie

she covers her face

he laughs

he goes to the hallway

she runs to stop him

JOHN   You have to let me go now /

IMOGEN   No you can't get out.

television up

he tries to move her gently

she pushes against him

he moves her more forcefully

she clings to him

she tries to kiss him

kiss me

he moves his face away

JOHN   stop

IMOGEN   hold me

JOHN   stop this now

IMOGEN   please

JOHN   stop, you have to stop now you have to stop now
              you have to give up now

he forces her away from the hallway

she clings to him

he pushes her away

he pushes her away

he goes down the hallway

she goes down the hallway and clings to his back

he pushes her away

he opens the door

he goes out the front door

he is gone

she stands on the threshold

she cannot pass the threshold

IMOGEN   it's not safe don't leave it's not safe it's not safe
don't leave me here it's not safe John I can't get
out and it's not safe John it's not safe

it isn't safe

she closes the door

she walks back down the hallway

enter IMOGEN.

IMOGEN *walks to the middle of the room.*

IMOGEN *turns around in a circle.*

Umm.

IMOGEN *crouches down and holds her head.*

IMOGEN *stands up and walks a few paces
towards the kitchen.*

And stops.

Umm.

Okay.

IMOGEN *walks back to the middle of the room.*

And stops.

IMOGEN *holds herself.*

IMOGEN *puts her hands to her head and walks a few paces.*

I am so angry. I am so so angry.

And stops.

IMOGEN *covers her face with her hands.*

IMOGEN *walks a few paces towards the TV room.*

And stops.

Okay. That's okay.

IMOGEN *bites her knuckles.*

IMOGEN *walks back again.*

And stops.

That is okay.

That is –

Everything is fine.

Everything is just fine and okay.

Umm

yes.

Yes.

That is how it is going to work.

Pause.

That is how it is going to work.

IMOGEN *goes and activates the art.*

She turns off the lights.

She sits in the execution room.

Silence.

Enter CHLOE.

CHLOE   Mum and Dad are crying. It's really weird.

          Pause.

          Where's John?

          Did he leave?

          Did he? Did he take his backpack with him?

          Oh.

          Silence.

          I lied. I totally would have fucked him. Whether
          he'd paid me or not. I don't know why I have to
          lie all the time.

          Do you think I'm a terrible person?

IMOGEN   Yes.

CHLOE   Bitch.

          Silence.

          Would you like to finish dinner?

          It's cold now anyway.

          It's all just cold now.

          Silence.

          Would you like to go into the garden with me?

          We could hold hands in the garden and listen to
          the world.

No.

I guess we shouldn't go outside until the
government says it's safe.

Silence.

Okay Immy, here's what I think has to happen.
We've all had a very difficult night, we're all in
shock, traumatised actually. And I think we all just
need to go to bed and have a nice rest. If we can't
sleep then we should just do something nice and
relaxing like drink some decaffeinated tea and read
a book. And in the morning we're all going to talk
about what happened outside. We're going to try
and understand what happened and how we feel
about what happened without making each other
afraid and without teaching each other to hate.
Because that's what Mum and Dad always did for
us, and that's what we're going to do together from
now on. As we're adults now, we're going to join in
this discussion because it is our responsibility, to
each other, to this country, and to the world. It is
our responsibility, and our privilege, to have this
discussion and try and understand what is
happening outside in the world, and be good
people, and be sympathetic and tolerant, and
open-minded, and apply our values and our beliefs,
which we hold very dearly, to this situation.

What do you think?

What do you think?

Immy?

Immy?

Pause.

IMOGEN   Something is going to happen.

Because it just keeps on happening.

You'll see.

Silence.

CHLOE   Right. Well.

I'll go and tell Mum and Dad the plan and get them to bed.

You just stay here, where it's safe.

Exit CHLOE, TV *room.*

IMOGEN *alone.*

The executions.

The TV softly softly there.

Silence.

Slow fade.

IMOGEN   Is he safe?

Can someone tell me if he's safe please?

I just want to know if he's safe. That is just all that I want to know.

So can someone tell me?

Please?

I just want to know if –

If someone could tell me –

Is he safe?

Is he?

Well is he?

Blackout.

Is he?

Is he?

Is he?

Is he?

Is he?

End.

My sweetly beloved, joy of my heart, I tell you this: truly, each one of us is guilty of the sins of all other men. I don't know how to explain this to you, but I feel the truth of it so deeply that it torments me.

The Karamazov Brothers, *Fyodor Dostoevsky*

A Nick Hern Book

One For Sorrow first published as a paperback original in Great Britain in 2018 by Nick Hern Books Limited, The Glasshouse, 49a Goldhawk Road, London W12 8QP, in association with the Royal Court Theatre, London

One For Sorrow copyright © 2018 Cordelia Lynn

Cordelia Lynn has asserted her right to be identified as the author of this work

Cover image by Root

Designed and typeset by Nick Hern Books, London
Printed in the UK by Mimeo Ltd, Huntingdon, Cambridgeshire PE29 6XX

A CIP catalogue record for this book is available from the British Library

ISBN 978 1 84842 761 7

CAUTION All rights whatsoever in this play are strictly reserved. Requests to reproduce the text in whole or in part should be addressed to the publisher.

Amateur Performing Rights Applications for performance, including readings and excerpts, by amateurs in the English language throughout the world should be addressed to the Performing Rights Manager, Nick Hern Books, The Glasshouse, 49a Goldhawk Road, London W12 8QP, *tel* +44 (0)20 8749 4953, *email* rights@nickhernbooks.co.uk, except as follows:

Australia: Dominie Drama, 8 Cross Street, Brookvale 2100, *tel* (2) 9938 8686, *fax* (2) 9938 8695, *email* drama@dominie.com.au

New Zealand: Play Bureau, PO Box 9013, St Clair, Dunedin 9047, *tel* (3) 455 9959, *email* info@playbureau.com

USA and Canada: Casarotto Ramsay and Associates Ltd, see details below

Professional Performing Rights Applications for performance by professionals in any medium and in any language throughout the world (including by stock companies in the USA and Canada) should be addressed to Casarotto Ramsay and Associates Ltd, Waverley House, 7–12 Noel Street, London W1F 8GQ, *fax* +44 (0)20 7287 9128, *email* agents@casarotto.co.uk

No performance of any kind may be given unless a licence has been obtained. Applications should be made before rehearsals begin. Publication of this play does not necessarily indicate its availability for amateur performance.

Woodland
CARBON
www.woodlandcarbon.co.uk
NICK HERN BOOKS
Printed on Carbon Captured paper

www.nickhernbooks.co.uk

facebook.com/nickhernbooks

twitter.com/nickhernbooks